understanding human behavior

An Illustrated Guide to Successful Human Relationships

COLUMBIA HOUSE / New York

Editor	Nicolas Wright
Deputy Editor	Susan Joiner
Senior Designer	Stewart Cowley
Art Editor	Mary Cooper
Art Assistant	Jeff Gurney
Editorial Assistants	Mundy Ellis
	Sarie Forster
	John Moore
	Michael McIntyre
Picture Research	Diane Rich
	Hazel Robinson
	Paul Snelgrove
Editorial Director	Graham Donaldson
Production Manager	Warren E. Bright

contents

introduction

There are few things more devastating for a child than being rejected by his parents. Rejection works in many ways; it ranges from callous indifference to extreme physical cruelty. But why do some parents behave in this way? And what happens to the child thus treated? Volume Nineteen of *Understanding Human Behavior* examines the child-rejection syndrome; it shows how a child's whole personality can be shaped by his first two years of life and it sounds a warning note: parents who reject their children are in turn rejected by them. They are ignored, rebelled against and finally in old age — when they need the support of their children most — they are left to fend for themselves.

We all swear — some of us more than others! In fact, swearing has become so commonplace that the words which once caused a shudder now don't even raise an eyebrow. The naughtiest words of yesteryear are so well established in our daily vocabulary that their effect is nil.

And yet, as you will learn from Volume Nineteen, though the effect of an expletive may have been lost, it is still subject to a great many social taboos. No matter how much we might swear ourselves we would be shocked to the core if a respected public figure suddenly let fly.

(continued)

Every time you drive your car you are contributing to a sequence of atmospheric changes which may cause the polar ice caps to melt and eventually flood the road you're driving on. Every time you throw away a plastic bag, flush detergent down the sink, or spray your garden with insecticide, you are helping upset nature's delicate balance.

Volume Nineteen of *Understanding Human Behavior* discusses pollution which—together with overpopulation—is possibly the greatest threat facing our own survival and, ultimately, the future of our frail planet. The solution lies with ourselves: the human element is still the decisive factor.

Students are always being criticized: they're dubbed sexually permissive, drug crazy and work shy. But how many people realize the strain most students are under. Volume Nineteen shows that the student's lot is not always the happy one it might at first appear.

—The Editor

BBC

Monkey business

Language is an ability which distinguishes man from other animals. But now that psychologists can successfully teach it to chimpanzees are we heading for the planet of the apes?

It is difficult to visualize a modern society without a spoken and written language. This ability distinguishes us from other animals which have evolved systems of communication. Yet, at the same time, it shows very clearly our affinity with less sophisticated creatures.

The ape, our nearest relative, can convey to other individuals his state of mind, emotions, moods, and desires. He cannot, however, relate abstract ideas; neither can he name objects or individuals around him. His verbal communications are simple, consisting of screams, hoots, grunts, chattering, and various other noises, none of which contain an element of speech. The main method of communication is by gesticulations and facial expressions. Indeed, the naked face of the ape has probably evolved to make facial expressions more easily visible.

Once more, our affinities are demonstrated by the similarities of facial expression between man and ape. The astonishingly mobile face of a chimpanzee often parodies human emotion. We are close enough to the ape to need no interpreter for such chimpanzee "language." The emotions and moods of the chimpanzee are made explicit to us by grimaces which almost exactly parallel those of a human in the same frame of mind.

Above: Washoe was brought up like a human by adults using only sign language. Now telling Dr. Roger Fouts she wants food is simply child's play.

This "primitive" part of human language is one which we still use to add force and nuances of meaning to our conversation. A slight smile, or a raised eyebrow, can impart a totally different meaning to the spoken word. And we can still use this faculty in the manner of an ape, without the aid of the spoken word. Parents often convey complex messages by grimacing and gesticulating, in the vain hope that their child will not comprehend.

Far from being in an evolutionary backwater as had long been assumed, it appears that chimpanzees in particular are still able to make advances in their mental evolution. In the wild, troops of chimpanzees have been observed to create simple tools, and have even improvized clubs with which to attack stuffed leopards, strategically placed by an experimenter. In other troops, the growth of an organized hunting technique has been noted. It may well be that at this point in their evolution, acquiring a language could help them make a giant evolutionary stride.

Both physically and mentally, the young chimpanzee and the human child have a great deal in common. They develop physically in a similar manner, and they acquire similar physical and mental skills. Examining the behavior of animals who parallel human development so closely may shed light on how we learn to talk.

Resonant Cavities

Early attempts at using chimpanzees as experimental models for human language learning proved a dismal failure, due to two basic misapprehensions. First, the animals were being taught to read detailed meanings into verbal sounds that normally have no meaning to chimpanzees, and more fundamentally, the chimpanzee's vocal apparatus is incapable of reproducing such complex sounds. Birds can be taught to speak, as opposed to talk, for they simply repeat words and phrases without any attempt to use them appropriately. But the chimpanzee can do neither, for it lacks the large resonant cavities in the mouth region which give our speech its richness; their vocal cords are different in structure and their tongue and palate do not lie in the same relative positions as ours. Despite these handicaps, success of a sort has been achieved.

In the 1940s a chimpanzee called Viki was raised as a member of the family by Keith and Cathy Hayes, who succeeded, after six years of intensive training, in teaching her to say four simple words: "mama," "papa," "up," and "cup." To an impartial observer, however, it is doubtful if these words would be recognizable. Earlier work showed that chimpanzees were quite capable of recognizing and understanding English words. In the 1930s, a couple named Kellogg raised a female chimpanzee called Gua together with their own child. At the age of 18 months, it was estimated that Gua understood 100 words,

although she never learned to speak.

Apart from the anatomical problems, another difficulty in teaching language to chimpanzees is that gesticulation is more natural to them than vocalization. In efforts to overcome the problem, more recent research has concentrated on the development of synthetic languages which can be used and understood by chimpanzees, and which take advantage of their natural tendencies. So far, three distinct "languages" have been created, all of which have proved highly successful and have caused many researchers to think again about our supposedly unique ability to use language.

Experience has shown that strict controls need to be built into any learning program to ensure that the animals are not simply picking up almost imperceptible cues from the trainer. This had proved to be the explanation for the success of a number of performing horses and dogs who appeared to be able to count, but in fact were provided with the answer by their trainer, quite unconsciously. A "talking" chimpanzee must be able to converse with anyone who has learned the language.

The most spectacular success has been achieved by Allen and Beatrice Gardner, both professors of psychology at the University of Nevada. They have taken advantage of observations made during the relatively unsuccessful attempts to teach Viki to speak intelligibly, when it was noted that each "word" was accompanied by a particular gesture. So the Gardners used an existing sign language—American Sign Language, or ASL. This sign language has been used for many years by the deaf and dumb. It has proved capable of expressing all of the complex nuances of the English language, and yet can be built up into a vocabulary, through a number of extremely simple stages, just as an infant learns normal spoken English. So the chimpanzee can itself select the items of language which it is able to grasp, exactly like a human child, and the researcher can make direct comparisons between the rate of learning in children and chimpanzees.

Deaf and Dumb Language

The Gardner's pioneering work began with Washoe, a female chimpanzee born in the wild, who was about a year old when her training began. Her physical and mental abilities were similar to those of a child of the same age. Washoe was treated almost exactly like a human

child. To avoid confusing her, the Gardners and their colleagues used only ASL when within earshot of Washoe, so she learned by copying them, in precisely the same way as would the child of deaf parents.

In ASL, each sign signifies a complete word, unlike finger spelling, which is another language used by the deaf. To a human, many signs are self-explanatory, such as that for baby (cradling the arms and rocking them from side to side) and for drink (clenching the fist with thumb extended and placing the thumb to the lips). Washoe seemed to find them equally obvious, for within less than a year she was stringing signs together into sentences, such as "Open food drink" to ask for a drink which she knew was in the refrigerator.

Spontaneous Sentences

Her ability to name an object or activity using signs was not unexpected; what was surprising was the ease with which she demonstrated an ability to transfer the name to other objects or situations, which she considered to be related. For example, Washoe was taught the sign for "open," which she used when she wanted the door of her room opened. But in rapid succession she transferred use of the sign to the refrigerator door, boxes, jars, drawers, and, more intelligently, to the water faucet. Obviously her concept of the meaning of "open" was precisely that of a normal human child.

Many of the more interesting insights into her learning abilities came from her mistakes. She was taught the sign for "flower," which she used correctly, and transferred to mean the odor of cooking or of tobacco. So she was taught "smell," and learned to differentiate the two. But she still sometimes confused "smell" and "flower"; perhaps indicating that a chimpanzee's idea of a pleasant smell is radically different from our own. Washoe showed a remarkable ability to recognize photographs of familiar objects, a very rare ability in animals. At first, she called them all "baby," but later showed that she also recognized them as the required object. "Baby" seems to mean "duplicate," or "model" in chimpanzee terms.

After 21 months of training, she had 34 signs which could be recognized by anyone conversant in ASL. By now

Chimpanzees use facial expressions to convey their feelings. Top right: A pout of greeting. Right: Teeth bared in a temper tantrum.

BBC

she had progressed to concepts rather than names, using signs like "funny" and "hurt" in the correct circumstances. Instead of tapering off, her learning rate now accelerated; within three years she knew 85 signs, and within another year nearly twice as many. She could now spontaneously produce sentences as complex as "Baby (doll) in my cup," using the individual signs in the appropriate order. Washoe had now mastered some simple rules of grammar as well as the signs for names and meanings.

At this stage in Washoe's education, she was handed over to Roger Fouts, another psychologist, at a research institute in Oklahoma. There she was introduced to other primates and

learned to call them "monkey." But when she was threatened by a rhesus monkey, he immediately became "dirty monkey," a remarkably human reaction. "Dirty" was a term she had previously used to describe her own feces, and just like many a human child she used the word with great glee. Another apt invention was her coining of the term "water bird" to describe a duck.

Washoe now has a number of colleagues being taught ASL, although at first she was disconcerted at the inability of other apes to understand her. Already, the beginnings of conversation between these young chimpanzees has been observed, although so far their vocabulary is too limited to

The language experiment with Washoe was successful because her teachers concentrated on communication, not sound.

allow much more than two-word "sentences." Some of these young chimpanzees have already shown an advance on Washoe's learning skills. The Gardners taught Washoe by showing her an object and simultaneously demonstrating the appropriate sign. But some of the chimpanzees at the institute already understood the names of many objects in spoken English. These animals learned to use a sign correctly when the trainer spoke the word and demonstrated the sign, without seeing the object. They were able to recognize an object visually, by spoken English (which is a totally alien and supposedly unattainable ability for a chimpanzee), and in ASL.

Lucy, another young chimpanzee at the institute, has her own pet, a ginger cat. Her games with the cat may have deep significance for the future study of language learning in the chimpanzee, for she attempted to teach the cat to use sign language. Lucy sat the cat in front of her, held up an object, and signed "what that" to the reluctant animal. With a cat, the response was nonexistent; with a chimpanzee infant, the result could have been dramatic.

Plastic Symbols

In complete contrast to the research initiated by the Gardners, with its adoption of a previously existing language with the same grammatical rules as English, other researchers have created artificial languages which they feel may be more appropriate to the intellectual capabilities of the chimpanzee. One such researcher is David Premack, of the University of California, Santa Barbara, who has trained Sarah, an African-born chimpanzee, with a "written" language. Sarah's language lessons began when she was about six years old, well past the equivalent age at which a human child most easily absorbs language.

Unlike Washoe, Sarah was not raised in a "family" environment, but lived and was taught in an ordinary laboratory pen. Washoe was continuously exposed to humans, as is a human infant, but Sarah had close human contact for only one hour a day, five days a week. Yet, despite this, she learned to master the language which Premack created for her, and, given the limitations under which she was trained, her accomplishments are remarkable.

Sarah's language consists of manipulating small colored plastic shapes on a magnetized board, arranging them in a vertical column. There are certain advantages to this system, in that the words or sentences constructed are semipermanent and not subject to the experimenter's interpretation, as must sometimes happen in the case of sloppily produced ASL. When a question is posed, Sarah remains aware of the problem, because it is on her work board—she cannot pretend that she has not noticed it.

Her education began in 1966, and she has since learned the meanings of about 130 of her plastic symbols.

Sarah's training was conducted by standard conditioning techniques. A stimulus was presented to her; if she responded correctly, she was rewarded; if a false response was offered, no reward was forthcoming, but she was not punished in any way. The meaning of the varied symbols was rapidly acquired, and Sarah went on to master simple rules of grammar and syntax, which Washoe used only in a rudimentary form.

By manipulation of her plastic symbols, Sarah has learned to ask questions, make plural constructions, and discuss abstract concepts. She has also learned to follow quite complex instructions, such as "Sarah insert apple pail Sarah insert banana disk," demonstrating that she can decide, by applying the appropriate grammatical rules, the exact sequence of operations she is being asked to follow.

About two years ago, Sarah's physical strength outgrew her trainers' determination to continue with her education. The training program is now continuing with two five-year-old chimpanzees, each of whom have so far learned to use about 50 signs. The question remains, Will they talk to each other? Unfortunately the spontaneity of ASL is lacking, and their conversation is more akin to that of deaf persons writing notes to each other with pencil and paper.

Yet another technique has been developed at the Yerkes Primate Research Center, in Atlanta. This program is conducted by Duane Rumbaugh of Georgia State University, who feels that although Washoe used combinations of words successfully, her understanding of the rules of grammar and syntax was not clear.

Punching the Keys

The Yerkes program revolves about Lana, a three-year-old chimpanzee who is being studied to learn the extent of her grasp of sentence meaning and structure, rather than her ability simply to learn names. Like Premack's Sarah, Lana spends her time in the laboratory, but her "tools" are much more sophisticated. Lana communicates by punching the 50 keys of a typewriter, which connects directly with a series of visual display screens and a PDP-8 computer. Every communication she makes is recorded by the computer, for later study.

Lana's learning and environment are all controlled by the computer. By punching the appropriate keys, she can request, "Please machine give piece of apple," followed by a symbol to indicate that she has completed the

message. As she types, the message is repeated on the illuminated display panel, where colored symbols matching those on the keys light up. If she makes her request accurately, the computer operates the machinery which drops a piece of apple into her feeding tray—or opens a viewing window, plays music, provides a drink, or whatever. If she makes an error, no reward is forthcoming. Lana then examines her message, deletes the offending words with a "cancel" button, and tries again.

Mobile Faces

There is no doubt that Lana can construct her own sentences correctly, but she can also correct "mistakes" made by the computer or the operator. When a part-sentence is typed into the visual displays by the operator, Lana will complete it accurately. If she considers the sentence to be inappropriate or inaccurate, she cancels it and then produces a corrected version.

These three totally different approaches to the problem of teaching chimpanzees to "talk" have shown their hitherto unsuspected abilities and demonstrated how their capacity to learn language closely parallels that of a human child. The gap between human and ape widens with increasing age, but this may result partly from the use of inappropriate languages, for it is likely that researchers have yet to hit upon the type of language most suited to the chimpanzee's personality. Indeed, it is possible that *we* would be unable to communicate with a chimpanzee in the language which comes to him most naturally. Unlike theirs, our human faces are not sufficiently mobile to communicate accurately highly complex messages solely by grimacing.

The next stage in research is to discover if chimpanzees will teach their own offspring the artificial language they have themselves been taught. Given time, would such a language spread spontaneously throughout a colony of chimpanzees? And more speculatively, if a colony of "talking" chimpanzees were returned to the wild, would their new ability to communicate with each other provide them with such an advantage over normal chimpanzees that they might become dominant by natural selection? If so, we could be providing an artificial spur to the evolution of the chimpanzee, which might result in the eventual appearance of another "intelligent" species.

Home sour home

They say there's no place like home, but when you're not wanted there it's not all peaches and cream. For the kid who's been discarded by his parents and thrown out with the garbage, life is more like a squashed tomato than the proverbial bowl of cherries.

There cannot be many worse fates for a child than to be born into a home where he is rejected by his parents. For many children, rejection means callous and indifferent neglect or positive hostility and cruelty from the parents. However, cruelty does not always take a physical form: it may be emotional and so subtle that the child comes to believe he is an unmitigated nuisance, that his very existence makes his parents unhappy, that he is something that is unwanted.

It is of vital importance for a child to identify with an adult and model himself on that adult's behavior. This means that he must form an attachment—a bond of love and dependency—with his parents. As the psychologists McCord and McCord put it, almost all social scientists believe that the development of conscience takes place primarily through the child's acceptance of his parents. The child and the parents strike an unconscious bargain: in return for the child's conformity to social restrictions, the parents give the child love. If the child fails to conform, he is momentarily rejected.

Unholy Alliance

In time, the child looks ahead to the consequences of his acts. If he is about to misbehave, a gnawing fear warns that his parents might stop loving him. Thus, the inner anxiety eventually results in internationalization of the parents' morality. The child has developed a conscience.

There is, of course, a more positive aspect to the formation of inner controls: not only does the child fear withdrawal of love, he also identifies with his parents. He loves them, and wishes to emulate them. As. personality theorist Gordon Allport has pointed out, children who fear the loss of love develop the concept of "must"; but the "ought" of behavior comes only through identification with parents and other moral symbols.

These developments are subverted if the parents fail to love the child. Parental rejection usually involves a combination of lax discipline and hostility. This unholy alliance produces very aggressive and poorly controlled behavior in the offspring. The lax parent is one who gives in to the child, acceding to his demands, indulging him, allowing him a great deal of freedom, being submissive and inconsistent and, in extreme cases, neglecting and deserting him.

Kim Sayer

The hostile parent is mainly unaccepting and disapproving of the child, failing to give affection, understanding or explanations. He or she tends to use a lot of physical punishment without giving reasons for exerting authority—something he does erratically and unpredictably. Over a long period of time this combination produces rebellious, irresponsible and aggressive children; they tend to be disorderly in the classroom and lacking in sustained concentration.

No Bonds

Psychologists have come to realize that extreme rejection or prolonged separations from mother or an adequate mother substitute (especially in the first two years of life when the child is becoming a social being) can have serious consequences for his personality development. The child psychiatrist Michael Rutter concludes from his exhaustive review of the evidence (in the book *Maternal Deprivation Reassessed*), "Distorted intrafamilial relationships involving both lack of affection and hostility or discord are associated with the development of later antisocial behavior and delinquency. Although the presence of a deviant parental model and inefficient discipline may be contributing factors, the lack of a stable, persistent, harmonious relationship with a parent appears to be the crucial variable.

"Less is known about the syndrome of 'affectionless psychopathy' but the little evidence available suggests that the most tenable hypothesis is that a failure to develop attachments (or bonds) in early childhood is the main factor. A bond to one or other parent, usually the mother, is the strongest attachment formed by most normal young children. Whether this is to the mother seems irrelevant in this connection and indeed it is doubtful whether it even has to be an adult."

Rejection, in its extreme forms, is an invidious kind of deprivation. The different forms of juvenile delinquency which have been related to different patterns of rejection include the unsocialized aggressive delinquent. This is the youth who is defiant of authority, malicious, sullen and characteristically hostile and coercive to the people around him, showing little guilt or remorse. Most often he comes from a family in which the parent-child relationships are filled with mutual suspicion, hostility and rejection. The parents punish severely and are inconsistent and unjust. It is difficult for the child to identify with

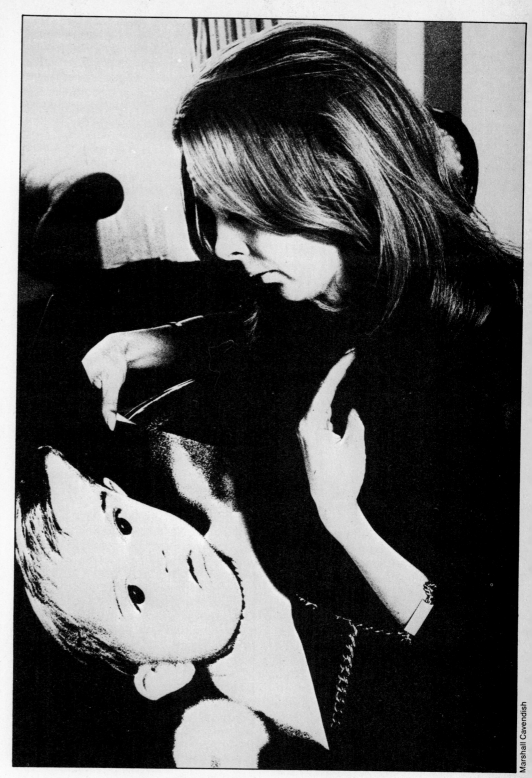

such parents, and thus the aggression they provoke is not directed against the self—as it is in the case of a child with a conscience—but is turned outwards on society.

Whereas punishments which evoke anxiety are likely to result later on in self-control, those producing an aggressive reaction in the child do not—though of course they may well make him wary of being caught. For this reason physical punishments are among the least effective as far as the development of the child's conscience

The mother who rejects her child at an early age may have regrets when he grows up a total stranger.

is concerned. The normal reaction to any physical assault is anger and aggression, though the expression of anger may be inhibited by fear.

Some parents reserve physical chastisement as a penalty for bullying. But a smacking is least suitable in this context if in the end the parent wishes the child to stop bullying, even when he cannot be found out. On the contrary, physical punishment may be confusing from the child's point of view. He is being beaten by a parent whom he is normally expected to imitate but who is now setting an example of the very behavior for which the child is blamed. As a general rule, physical punishment stimulates feelings of aggression. It bypasses the more subtle sense of anxiety which results in resistance to temptation by self-control not fear of punishment.

Phantom Parents

It is almost a law of human nature that punishment leads to self-control only when the child is on the side of the person punishing. Since he loves his mother, the child is partly on his mother's side. Because of this identification with his mother, he will share her condemnation of himself. In the case of a loveless child this assumption cannot be made. Although loving attachment makes the development of conscience possible, it also places in the hands of the mother a power which could be detrimental to the child. If a child is strongly and exclusively attached to a mother who sets impossibly high standards and is deeply "hurt" when her child fails to live up to them, it is probable that the child will acquire a sense of conscience so severe and restrictive that his instincts are crippled and much of his creative energy will remain unused.

Parental rejection takes many forms. Abandonment is an extreme form of rejection and is only too often the fate of illegitimate children, though this is not necessarily the case. A study of a thousand unmarried mothers in California showed that they were fairly representative, socioeconomically, of all females of equivalent age, race, and marital status in that state. The majority of the mothers reported either a love relationship or a close friendship with their sexual mates, who also seemed quite typical of men in general. The personalities of the mothers ranged from very positive to very negative, but the majority represented the norm for females of similar age and showed little evidence of subnormal mentality or emotional instability. In fact, the only thing that unmarried mothers seem to have in common is an illegitimate child.

There has been a dramatic liberalizing of social attitudes, as well as public policies, in many countries during the twentieth century. But however liberal the present-day policies may be, there are serious personal problems remaining for the child of the unmarried mother. The

illegitimate child is made to feel different. He may hear certain insinuations: "after all, he wasn't wanted by them," "he was a mistake," or "he's their punishment." These stereotyped attitudes may be only unconsciously felt, but they can still have a profound influence on the sensitive child's growing self-esteem.

To those who have grown up within a family it is nearly impossible to comprehend fully what it must be like to know nothing of one's family—either of one parent (if the mother keeps the child) or both of them (if the child is placed in care). Diana Dewar, introducing her book *Orphans of the Living*, describes this lack of a sense of family as the greatest human grief apart from death—when forlorn, loveless children mourn for phantom parents. The problem is mitigated to a large extent when illegitimate babies have substitute parents, as in adoption, but there are many more illegitimate children of all races than childless couples who want to provide a family life for them.

Many illegitimate children accept the popular myth (and stigma) that they come from "bad blood." One of the most difficult handicaps of all for them to bear is their feeling of inferiority, of being unwanted by at least one parent (if not both). And another burden is the lack of a family history to give them a niche in society. Boys find it much harder than girls to accept that their mother was unmarried when they were born and never married their father. In these matters, the truth has a way of coming out, and if it is not explained to a child in a humane and sensitive way, it may come out in a crude jest or some other traumatic discovery.

Dog in the Manger

Those children whose mothers have no hope of making a home, or who may not even wish to acknowledge the baby, remain the hard core of youngsters in long-term care. The extramarital offspring of married women are often admitted to orphanages because the husband will "forgive" his wife her unfaithfulness only if she gives up the child. These are often very sad cases, since the mothers sometimes have strong maternal feelings and agree to part with the new baby only to preserve the home for the children of the marriage. Later on, such children may long to be in touch with their mothers but the husbands will seldom allow this, even after many years.

The illegitimate child who suffers

most is the one whose future home is continually undecided, usually because of the unstable personality of the mother. She may tenaciously hang onto the child as a symbol of the wrong she feels has been done her. On the other hand, she may have convinced herself, no matter how unlikely the prospects, that she will one day sort things out and make a satisfactory home for the child. In the meantime the child may suffer from severe early emotional deprivation, never knowing a real home. Many countries have introduced legislation to protect children from the mother who fails to assume a maternal role but will not permit anyone else to do so.

Struggle to Survive

There is a familiar pattern in the lives of this type of mother and child. The mother had an unhappy childhood (perhaps being illegitimate herself) and no loving parents to stand by her when she was in trouble. Feeling herself an outcast, she has to face up to the responsibility of a child when her way of life shows her she is incapable of being responsible for herself. She is probably torn between a desire to shelve her burdens and have the baby adopted and an even greater desire to possess at least one human being to love and be loved by in return. She compromises, finding some way to keep the child and at the same time work to support him. She is likely to stay in lodgings where a landlady or registered child-minder cares for him while she is at work, but lodgings of this kind are hard to come by and difficult to keep. She may use a day nursery. If the child gets sick and she has to take time off from work, she could lose her job. Then living on some form of welfare, she may slide into debt. If the rent is not paid, she could end up on the street.

There are several courses of action at this point, such as a casual liaison with a man or prostitution—both tragic for her own and the child's well-being. If she is not successful in finding alternative accommodation or resources quickly, she may give up the struggle of keeping the child with her. He will end up in care, torn from the small bit of security he has so far known. This may be the last the child sees of the mother. She may, however, struggle to get him back, and visit him regularly at the children's home with presents and treats. Only too often these visits become less regular or taper off completely.

Children in this situation may show great loyalty to the rejecting parent and weave elaborate fantasies as to why she cannot visit and when they will be reunited. The effects of such instability and insecurity on a child's life are incalculable.

Most social workers, in the course of their work, come into contact with the problems of the neglected child, the youngster who is a victim of emotional deprivation.

"Failure to thrive" is a sociologist's term describing the result of parental neglect and physical abuse, yet another aspect of a breakdown in the mothering function. There have been reports of deliberate withholding of food from children; recent studies in hospitals draw attention to the fact that there is a regular, though small, incidence in hospital admissions of babies under the age of three years who repeatedly return to hospital for failure to thrive and develop properly, or with broken limbs or severe internal and external bruising.

As early as 1946 a connection between fractures of the long bones and severe head injuries in children was noted by a radiologist, but it was another six years before it was accepted that these were not accidents. Dr. Silverman, American radiologist, reported, "Many individuals responsible for the care of infants and children (who cannot give their own history) may permit trauma, but forget or be reluctant to admit it, or may deliberately injure the child and deny it." But apart from scattered reports, it was not until the early 1960s that further research was undertaken and given publicity.

In general there was a good deal of complacency—despite the publicizing of a few notorious and tragic cases of child deaths—in connection with this serious form of child abuse. It was for this reason that Professor Henry Kempe (coeditor of the book *Helping the Battered Child and his Family*) used the emotive term "battered child." In June, 1972, in the *British Medical Journal,* Dr. Graham Jackson at King's College Hospital, London, reported on the tendency for medical personnel still to overlook the syndrome. He reported his findings in one hundred case records of children aged two or less, admitted for physical injury. When cases where the cause of the injury was clear were excluded, eighteen children still remained. According to Dr. Jackson, in each of these eighteen cases there was enough objective evidence to suggest a strong possibility that the child was being abused, but this diagnosis seems not to have been considered.

Double-edged Weapon

The battered baby syndrome is no new phenomenon, but an awareness of its extent, in possibly all strata of society, is only now dawning. Many of the causal factors in this problem can be traced to the parents' own childhood, uncovering a cycle of deprivation. Physically violent parents have often suffered severe emotional deprivation themselves and have had their dependency needs frustrated. As a result many grow up unable to nurture their offspring or to empathize with them; they tend to be highly dependent and very low in self-esteem. Many of the parents of battered children have personality disorders ranging from extreme emotional immaturity and neurosis to psychopathy.

Rejection, of course, is a double-edged weapon. Parents who reject their children are rejected by them in turn. Eventually they are ignored, rebelled against, and even abandoned by their unhappy youngsters, so that in their old age these unstable parents lose the one prop that might make their lives worth living.

Sun Gravure

Little girl lost: a child who is not loved by her parents may withdraw and have difficulty making friends.

Liz Moyes

The madding crowd

Multiplication—that's the name of the game, but if we go on like this we will soon be standing shoulder to shoulder, fighting for food and a breath of fresh air.

The population explosion presents one of the greatest threats ever to face mankind. The very word "population" is almost invariably linked with other words like "problem," "crisis," "dilemma," "emergency."

The mere number of people on this earth is not only a problem in itself, but it is also the root cause of most of the other evils with which humanity has to grapple on a world scale—pollution, lack of resources and energy, starvation, poverty, disease, crime, war, and the many other scars on the face of civilized life. It is hard to face the facts and figures and remain neutral and dispassionate; they turn you into an alarmist and propagandist. The simple fact is there are already far too many people on this planet.

This seems an absurd impression to the man who leaves his home in a spacious suburb and gets on a plane which flies him over mile upon mile of open countryside. How can he equate what he sees with the predictions of the doomsayers who warn that every habitable part of the globe has already been settled, and that by the end of the next century we will be standing shoulder to shoulder? The aircraft cabin is probably the worst possible viewpoint from which to contemplate the population problem. It belies the facts of the matter, facts which mean different things to different people.

To the demographer—the statistician with his charts, graph, and slide rule—the overpopulation problem is a set of figures confronting him with an insoluble equation. The figures, which are out-of-date before they are even collated, show that there are nearly 4 billion people in the world and that 75 million are added every year. It was not until 1650 that we reached our first half-billion, and the next 300 years brought 2 billion more—around 2.5 billion in 1950. But the next two billion, so it is predicted, will take only a tenth of that time—4.5 billion in 1980. At the present growth rate we should have a population of 6.5 billion by the turn of the century, possibly reaching 8 billion less than ten years after that.

Breaking Point

What appear to be the wildest prognostications are rooted in these facts. One of them comes from a British physicist who calculates that before the end of the next century there will be 60 billion people spread over the globe; that is 100 per square yard of the earth's land and sea surface. This is obviously an inconceivable situation, and breaking point will have been reached long before that. Already we cannot feed our present population adequately. There are limits to the amount of space available and obstacles to the fair distribution of food, materials and energy. The only unlimited capacity we have seems to be in reproducing our species. This is the statisticians' insoluble equation.

For the affluent suburban man of the wealthier nation, the population problem means the "agony" of rush-hour travel, urban congestion, the "misery" of shopping on Christmas Eve, going on waiting lists, and the occasional shortage of some consumer commodity. It is a mild inconvenience. But these are the things which bring the problem home to him rather than the Sunday paper reports on how the other half lives, or television documentaries which can be switched off.

But for these others—the majority of the world's population—the crisis is a stark reality. Half the world is hungry and several million people—mostly children—die of starvation every year, the victims of famine or natural disaster. From the rural areas of India and Ethiopia to the shanty towns of Calcutta or Jakarta survival is the best life can offer. The problem is the same: too many people and not enough to go around. It takes a walk down an Indian city street for even the most enlightened demographer to begin to "get the feel" of the real magnitude of the problem.

It is not just a matter of numbers alone, or the allocation of people to a given number of square miles. This is what the air traveler, zooming over acres of uninhabited open space, would fail to take into account. The problem arises because every person has to be fed, clothed, and sheltered, a task which the world's present resources—and the economic systems by which they are produced and distributed—cannot adequately perform. People also need to be educated, they need health and welfare services, they need jobs and demand exceeds supply.

Our present resources are not up to the job, and in the absence of either an unpredictable catastrophe which would effectively reduce numbers, or a miracle of science which would unearth new resources, the future promises a situation in which twice as many people are using up half the resources. The steps we are taking about it now are at best stopgap contingency measures to deal with the present emergency: we cannot put much by for the future.

Imbalance of Nature

Another illusion held by our air passenger is that the populations of the world are evenly spread over the landmasses of the globe. If they were, he might see more people scattered around the vast wasteland area which his view commands. But some countries are crammed to saturation point while others, like parts of Africa and South America, reckon themselves to be deficient. Geographical and climatic factors make other places utterly uninhabitable. The expanses of open space in the saturation countries of Asia are accounted for by people's migration from the rural areas and their concentration in the cities.

By an accident of history the earth is now divided into two parts. One is composed of the developed countries, the wealthy nations with advanced technologies, like North America, Europe, the U.S.S.R., Japan and Australasia. The other consists of the rest—the poor countries, undeveloped and not so much as self-sufficient in resources. The imbalance of nature also endows these poorly provided nations with far more than their fair share of the world's population. They are caught in a vicious circle; as long as they lag behind in industrial development, go short of materials and energy, and maintain poor medical and educational services—which taken together create the conditions which favor small families—the population will be ever-increasing.

Redistribution of Resources

The developed nations are made up of about one-third of the total world population. The growth rate—the percentage of births over deaths—averages at about 1 percent a year in the biggest two nations, the United States and the U.S.S.R. In the undeveloped countries live the remaining two-thirds. Their growth rate, however, is 2.5 percent, and in some places as high as 3.4 percent. At this rate they will have to accommodate 5½ billion people by the end of this century, 28 billion fifty years later, and adding a billion a year by the end of next century. At present the peoples of these countries consume 8 times less per head than do the people of developed nations. Another estimate claims that the average Westerner is eating into the world's pool of resources 500 times faster than, say, an Asian living on the breadline.

These few statistics are enough to show that, in considering population problems, you have two sets of figures to deal with: one tells a story of glaring poverty, the other of unashamed affluence. The disparity of population density may not have been the initial cause of the discrepancy between living standards of the two groups, but it has certainly exaggerated the problems. We know that 30 percent of the world's population consumes 75 percent of its resources. On the one hand we have vast populations eking out a meager existence on poor resources, or starving for complete lack of them. On the other hand we have affluent nations with overfed populations, huge surpluses, and appalling waste. This is the problem.

On the face of it, the answer looks simple. You just channel the surplus to the countries which do not have enough and if that still fails to meet the demand you constrain the wealthy nations at least not to consume more than they need. Then you have even distribution of resources. But we should not think of resources as some single substance which can be packaged and transported from places where it is in excess to places where it is in short supply. Even if this were so there would be no reason to think that the problem had been solved. The problem is overpopulation, and any humanitarian gesture to redeploy supplies will not solve it.

Another obstacle to any easy solution is human nature. Over the centuries man has come to think of himself as a member of separate ethnic or national groups living apart from others. In the days before he had explored his planet to its limits and before developments in science and communications made global and international activity possible, that was good enough. But now he has to think of himself as a member of the whole human race—a great responsibility to have thrust on him all of a sudden. Wherever he is, his activities have direct repercussions in the far corners of the earth. But he is as irrational as ever; life is still arranged so that a man in a wealthy nation can consume twice as much as he needs in the full knowledge that someone on the other side of the world is starving, while the undernourished man will go on having children in total disregard of the certainty that he will be unable to provide for them.

Reproduction is a basic human urge. At one time having large families presented the only hope for the survival of the species. High infant mortality, short life expectancy, and the ever present hazards of life—disease, famine, war, accident, overexertion—compounded to make a higher deathrate than birthrate a very real possibility. Evolution by natural selection allowed only for the survival of the fittest. We are descended from those with the greatest resistance to the calamities of life and we have inherited their high degree of immunity. We also issue from those with the greatest capacity to reproduce, and we are endowed with that too.

Science Plays Its Part

Long after the survival of the human race was assured there was a remarkable leap forward in medical science. This, according to population expert Dr. Paul Erlich, was the straw which broke the camel's back. It happened about 1800 when populations, in the developed countries at least, stood at a level which promised a decent standard of living for all. It lowered the infant mortality rate, reduced the number of deaths due to disease and injury, arrested the process of aging, and lengthened the span of years in which a woman could be expected to reproduce. Meanwhile the march of science and technology took much of the donkey work out of life, which became less hard and lasted longer.

Forgetting for the moment that medical science can be applied to the reduction of population, we can see that together with our strong sexual urge and the generous allocation of fertile periods in the female reproductive system, advances in medicine have made propagation harder to avoid than to achieve. This is where man's other unique genetic endowment might have come in useful—his capacity for rational thought and intellectual appraisal of his predicament for exercising some measure of control over his destiny. But in this matter it did not. Mankind has gone on reproducing as though he had no thought for tomorrow.

Return of the Four Horsemen

The first authoritative warnings of the dangers of uncontrolled population growth came from the social economist Thomas Malthus in about 1800, although the subject had been previously broached by Franklin and Hume. Malthus' pessimistic treatise *An Essay on the Principle of Population* pointed out the natural tendency of populations to increase faster than their means of subsistence. With man, he said, propagation could be controlled by reason, although the ultimate check was want of food. It could be prevented by moral restraint and by prophylactic methods but, failing that, other factors would emerge to discourage population growth or to reduce numbers: unwholesome occupations, severe labor, extreme poverty, bad nursing, large towns, excesses of all kinds, diseases, wars and famine.

On reading Malthus' work, Charles Darwin said that natural selection was an inevitable result of rapid increase of all organic beings, as such a rapid growth in numbers necessarily leads to a struggle for existence. But the intensity of that struggle was considerably mitigated by breakthroughs in science, technology, and agriculture, which were occurring at that time in response to the social demands. They confounded Malthus' gloomy prophecy that "the power of population is so superior to the power of the earth to produce subsistence to man that premature death must in some shape visit the human race."

The stages of a population explosion are very simple. Once you have a sudden upward swing, a snowballing process has started which only some catastrophe can significantly reverse. Plain for all to see is the fact that on the whole children outnumber parents. From there on it is a matter of elementary arithmetic. A man with two children has, in numerical terms, reproduced himself and his wife. A number of grandchildren and even great-grandchildren will be born before he himself dies, by which time he will have reproduced himself many times over. If the birthrate exceeds the deathrate the population continues to grow—and the longer this situation persists the faster that growth proceeds, as each generation provides a broader base for the creation of the next.

A growth rate of 1 percent doubles a population in 70 years, 2 percent doubles it in 35 years, 3 percent in 23 years, and so on, assuming that everybody survives and not allowing for deaths by famine, war, accident, disease or misadventure which on a large scale relieve the situation. This rate does not take into account immigration and emigration, male-female ratios, and so on, which obviously have a bearing on any population statistics within any given country.

In the United States, where the rate of growth is as modest and well controlled as anywhere in the world, it is felt that an ideal situation would be achieved if every couple limited itself to two children. If this were achieved, by some having more and others less, it would not be until the end of the next century that the country's population would stabilize, when it would stand at between 370 and 400 million. If it could be achieved throughout the world, by about the year 2040, the total world population would level off at just under 16 billion, over four times greater than today.

Pessimistic Predictions

Just as the world can be subdivided into two, so each nation can, in a sense, be regarded as two nations—the rural population and the city dwellers. In the developed countries, 80 percent of the population live in towns, and in the undeveloped nations, the migration into the urban centers is steady and unrelenting. It is estimated that by 1980 3½ billion will be living in the cities of these countries.

Aristotle once said that people came to the cities in search of the "good life." That may have been true in his day, but now it is importunity which drives them there and which their new environment does little to relieve. They come in search of jobs for themselves and education for their children, or they come just to stay alive.

Every city is in reality two cities: each has its affluent, fashionable central areas and its elegant suburban fringes, but it also has its slum areas, its twilight zones and shanty towns.

It is here that the majority of migrants converge in far greater numbers than can be absorbed. They have to be fed, employed, educated, transported, entertained. It is in the cities that the problems of overpopulation are most harshly felt. Overcrowding makes for problems of health, sanitation, and hygiene. Health and welfare services are often overwhelmed by the persistent influx of people and can do little to maintain a decent standard of living. Unable to provide enough resources, housing, education, medical care or employment, they fight a losing battle against the deterioration of conditions, and the way is left wide open for the increase of crime, violence, squalor, vagrancy, poverty, hardship, and all the concomitant ills of overcrowded conditions.

This is happening now, and a recent survey has shown how much more likely to increase are the populations of the cities which are at present most densely inhabited. Djakarta, a city in Indonesia built for two million people, already has four million. It tops the table of projected growth with a 93 percent increase by 1985. By then, Calcutta, which now has a population of nearly 7 million, will have swelled its numbers by 75 percent. Tokyo's projected increase will bring its population to over 25 million. How will these people be living then?

Like rats? This may not seem too wide of the mark if we consider how rats do live in overcrowded conditions. A few years ago an American psychologist, John B. Calhoun, conducted a series of extensive experiments with a confined rat population. For a time he allowed the population to increase at its natural rate. When it reached a manageable limit, it stabilized. What might have expanded to a colony of 5,000 animals in the prescribed time span remained at 150. But this was not achieved as a result of any wisdom or forbearance on the part of the rats.

Sardines in a Can

The stabilization was the result of their violent perversion of the course of nature. Most of the deaths were due to the negligence of the mothers, who refused to build nests for their young or deserted them if they did. Other deaths were due to fierce territorial contests between males, and some to cannibalism. What was left of the colony became either unnaturally aggressive, paranoid, withdrawn, overdefensive, hyperactive, sexually perverted or generally neurotic.

What Dr. Calhoun had done was to create a miniature overcrowded city. Even with the added advantage of reason and intelligence, man has done little better in his congested environment than his rodent counterpart. We have a natural psychological aversion to living at too close quarters and do not remain sociable in this predicament for long. Figures for acts of violence, crime, arson, sexual perversion, suicide and other disruptive behavior are higher per capita for the densely populated cities than elsewhere: they are daily occurrences. As with the rats, violent, antisocial and wayward behavior becomes the norm.

Whichever way you look at it, the population explosion appears to have set us on a course for self-destruction —economic, biological, psychological, social, and environmental. Man's struggle for existence has always involved maintaining the balance between the demands of populations and the supply of the earth's natural resources. Until that equilibrium is achieved something has got to give. We can either reduce the rate of population growth, or allow it to increase and reduce the standard of living for all or increase the yield of nature. At present, the burden of overpopulation is being met in all three ways: some populations are being allowed to die; others are condemned to a pitifully impoverished standard of living; others are turning the full force of technology into an assault on the land to maximize its produce. Ultimately, man's survival depends on how long his natural environment can hold out.

David Levin/Jancis Cowley

Too many demands are being made on the world's limited resources: soon our nest egg may crack.

Ron Embleton

Birds and bees

All too often sex education just means passing on one generation's hang-ups to the next.

Throughout history, the typical family has lived in no more than one or two rooms, in many cases sharing their beds or sleeping mats. Some of the more primitive tribes still do. Children brought up under these circumstances have no embarrassment or ignorance about the human body. By comparison, people in the developed nations suffer great inhibitions, ritually concealing their bodies from each other, segregating the sexes, and assigning different activities to certain rooms.

In Western society, children in peasant communities are traditionally less inhibited about sex and the human body. Any child brought up in the country is likely to pick up facts about the nature of sexual activity from the mating of farm animals.

The habits of European rural society towards the end of the nineteenth century shocked Scottish novelist Robert Louis Stevenson. On a walking tour of rural France (reported in his *Travels with a Donkey*) he found that innkeepers assumed that he would share a bedroom with others. And on the first occasion, to his embarrassed astonishment, he found that one of his compulsory bedroom companions was a woman—he was to share a room with a married couple and their small child. One bed for them, the other for him. "I kept my eyes to myself, and knew nothing of the woman except that she had beautiful arms, and seemed no whit embarrassed."

The compartmentalization of everyday activities within the Western home

is relatively recent. Before the industrial revolution, the family home was also often the "unit of production"—some or all of the produce for sale or for the family's own needs, was made at home, by both men and women. The center of domestic activity was the hall of the house, the entrance space. Meals were cooked there, some of the family slept there, and some sort of productive labor was done there. In England, separate rooms for separate activities—a cooking room, sleeping rooms, and so on —were not common in working-class homes until towards the end of the nineteenth century.

A Western child now experiences many barriers in the home. He (or she) is unlikely to have seen his parents naked; probably he has never slept in the same room with them; nor, perhaps, has he ever seen other children's bodies—if, as is typical, he is a member of a small family. He almost certainly has to be formally instructed about the nature of the human body, its changes as it matures, and the sexual act. And he is likely to feel great shock and temporary disbelief at the thought of his parents indulging in an activity so alien to all he knows about them.

In most of the world's societies, sex "education" is a more automatic process than it is in Western industrial societies. The anthropologist Margaret Mead, who has carried out extensive studies into the behavior of primitive societies, suggests that a child needs to be able to observe the constant, gradual physical changes among many other children, adolescents and adults.

Early Awareness

"What the child receives in a primitive society," she writes, "is the assurance that there is a continuous series of steps between his small body and that of an adult. The little boy needs to see the changes in body form and hair, the gradually developing genitals . . . the first soft facial down." To see these things will bind his sense of himself to the man he will become.

And the little girl, Dr. Mead feels, needs to be able to observe, and to identify with, a series of girls—from "the nubile girl with budding breasts to the mature young woman, and finally to the just pregnant, the fully pregnant, and the postparturient and suckling mother. This is what happens in those primitive societies in which the body is hardly covered at all. . . . The full pageant of human development from early childhood to full maturity is visible."

In primitive societies, the child is, as it were, surrounded by continuous sex education. A lot of the ceremony and celebration in tribal life is concerned with sexual matters, and children hear and see explicitly sexual behavior between adults. Accustomed to this from the first, sexual knowledge is acquired gradually.

In some societies where the virginity of a bride is important, proof of her virginity is shown publicly. A woman who is a virgin has a thin membrane covering the entrance to the vagina, and the first penetration of the vagina will break this membrane and often cause a drop or two of blood to be shed. After the couple have gone to their marriage bed, in some societies, a large white cloth stained with blood will be hung outside the house, as "proof" of the bride's virginity (a practice of doubtful value: cheating with chicken blood is commonly contrived).

Girls and boys growing up with such customs must acquire sexual knowledge as a matter of course. Some societies praise the sexual parts of a child's body very early. Dr. Mead cites the Balinese, who tease a baby boy's penis, crying, "Handsome, handsome, handsome," as they do so, and pat a little girl's vulva gently, crying, "Pretty, pretty, pretty." And a little girl of two or three walking with her belly thrust out might be poked playfully and teased about being pregnant.

The passing from childhood to maturity is also almost invariably a matter for celebration in primitive societies. In many societies there is a specific time at which a boy is understood to become a man and when he must pass initiation tests to be admitted to manhood. And whereas in Western society a girl's first menstruation is usually a matter for secrecy, embarrassment, and shame, in primitive societies the occasion is usually marked with a public celebration. A girl is also liable to be betrothed some years before menstruation. Sometimes she goes to live with her "husband's" family, both of them fully accepting of their future together, both waiting unquestioningly for sexual maturity and the correct time for their actual mating.

Although people in such societies enjoy what seems to us a lot of sensuous freedom, untainted by shame, in fact their taboos and strictures are very strong. Some societies, for instance, prohibit sexual intercourse while a wife is nursing a child —and since she may nurse him for three years, this is a considerable restriction. Every society has its rules.

A child in a primitive society may have to learn complicated gradations governing his behavior with other people, according to their relationship to him. Rules governing sexual relationships are complicated and incest taboos particularly stringent. A boy avoiding proscribed contacts with a "sister" may find that a third of the girls of the village fit into this category, though genealogical "records" are so unreliable and bewildering that it may be difficult for a man to be sure whether a particular woman is in a forbidden relationship to him or not.

Changes in life at adolescence are sometimes as difficult as in our own society. Initiation tests for boys are often very demanding, sometimes painful. There can be pain for girls, too, as in one society's ceremonies surrounding a girl's first menstruation, in which the older women of her family instruct her in rolling stinging nettle leaves and inserting them into

There was no room for privacy or modesty in the average family home of only a century ago.

Radio Times

An initiation ceremony in Ghana. In many primitive societies a boy becomes a man in the space of a few hours of public ritual.

her vulva to make her breasts grow.

Restriction and inhibition at puberty are taught particularly to the girl. She learns protective measures like keeping her legs crossed or tucking her heels under her; she must dress to protect her sexual areas, with a grass skirt carefully concealing her; she will probably tend more and more to be chaperoned.

Boys may also suffer a sudden loss of freedom. Margaret Mead writes of one New Guinea society in which, after a carefree childhood, boys in their early teens are whisked away to be initiated: then they may spend several miserable months, or sometimes years, during which they are chased away by the women, though they are not yet anxious to join the men. In one society, boys are sent away in early childhood to their maternal grandparents to lead a life of ease; then, when the time for initiation arrives, they are sent back to encounter the harshness of a father to push them into manhood.

In any society, the pattern of social organization is what trains a child in his social and sexual behavior and his expectations of the behavior of others. And different societies have very different patterns of social organization. In some, there is little emphasis on distinctions between men and women. Boys and girls play the same games; fathers show tenderness to children; sexual relationships may be initiated by females as well as by males; dominance and competitiveness are not admired, and neither are violence and aggression.

In another society, both men and women may be expected to be violent and aggressive, children may be treated harshly, and there may be hostility and competition within the family—between parents and children, between man and woman. And again, elsewhere, women may be taught to be self-reliant, dominant, and sexually aggressive, while the men are relaxed and submissive. Most peoples lie somewhere between these extremes, and their "sex-education"—one of the ways a society conveys its own nature to its children—reflects this considerable variation.

The Samoan culture and its ap-

proach to sex was the one which Margaret Mead considered particularly desirable. Samoans expected sex to be a delightful experience, and unashamedly considered sexual expertise a desirable skill. They disapproved of great passions, however, regarding them as threats to the social order. Parents did not discuss sex with children, although parents and children might together attend dances of uninhibited frankness. As a girl became ready for sexual experience, she would be chosen for her first love affair by an older boy, who had himself been initiated into full sexual experience by older girls. Marriages were arranged between families, though the parents would take the wishes of the young people into consideration as well, and thereafter the girl was expected to become pregnant only by her betrothed, although this must sometimes have turned out to be wishful thinking. Children were treated indulgently, but without any passionate or possessive mother-child relationships and marriages were stable. Samoans were also able to adjust to change, weaving Christianity lightly into the fabric of the native culture without damage.

In marked contrast to the Samoan culture, Margaret Mead notes modern society's difficulty in absorbing change into its attitudes to sex. "In a changing society, the parts of the system get out of step; a childhood suited for an expressive adolescence may be followed by a restricted one, or a restricted childhood be followed by a demand for an expressive adolescence. Then the patterns become confused; more children fail to experience the sequence of events which, in that culture, are the appropriate prelude to adulthood."

Element of Choice

When, as today, procreation is no longer accepted as the sole purpose of adult life, and the biological purpose of sexual intercourse is no longer its sole function, establishing and passing on sexual values becomes very difficult: simple certainties disappear. The fact that a future of pregnancies is no longer the morally approved future for a woman puts painful elements of choice and decision making into sex education. The small girl in a primitive society sees all about her examples of the single norm for adult women. In an urban, industrial society, the small girl sees adult women living in a variety of ways: some of them unmarried, some of them childless—and some of them apparently achieving status or fulfillment in spite of this.

It may indeed be comfortable to have a single norm of behavior in a society. But it is impossible to transplant customs evolved within a simple, exclusive culture into a complex, industrial, literate and mobile society, where people tend to question simple, time-honored assumptions. At the same time, medicine has greatly increased life span and saves millions of babies that would otherwise die. A responsible woman in an industrial society cannot regard herself as nothing but a baby machine—if for no other reason than that within a very brief time the country's population would reach untenable proportions. The modern child needs to know that contraception can give him control over the size of his future family, and that this control is necessary for the sake of social order.

Fertility is Not Enough

Sex education regarding contraception is more difficult in industrial societies in another way: in primitive societies, if a man is fertile, he is sexually successful. Now, fertility is not enough, because as a rule the couple will want only two children. With contraception, the purpose of sexual intercourse is demonstrably one of pure pleasure and love, and the man must consider his lover's pleasure, must learn sexual skill. Plentiful evidence showing that women have, if anything, a greater capacity for orgasm than men feeds this obligation. Many men, with either puritan or domineering attitudes towards women, find this difficult to face: for them, a wife who rejoices in sexual intercourse, and experiences orgasm, is not entirely desirable. Some women, with either puritan or submissive attitudes towards men, feel the same way. Contraception, for some, has destroyed the "moral" reason for the sensual act.

Western society has inhibited sensuality—touching each other is largely forbidden in almost every social situation, except in very small children. Margaret Mead refers to the "lack of skin sensuousness of Americans" and attributes to this the great emphasis on looks and appearance in American love and love-making. This visual emphasis multiplies the difficulties resulting from the way we conceal our bodies. We hide erogenous areas,

A relaxed attitude to nakedness and sexuality is an important part of informal sex education.

PAF International

forbid touching, deny sensuality, and yet expose children to extraordinary gigantic, technological versions of the female body—an endlessly repeated breast-and-thigh diet of visual erotica on television screens, in advertising, and in sexual fantasy films—most of them recreating "primitive" male and female stereotypes.

Redress the Balance

It seems that we have contrived a peculiarly difficult society which combines a prohibition of sensuous contact between most people with a life-long visual stimulus of sexual desires. It may be that we need to adjust the balance, to reduce belief in the importance of sexual achievement and relearn sensuous contact between people in normal everyday social situations.

Writing on psychosexual development, William Simon and John H. Gagnon suggest that the power of sexuality may have been promoted and overemphasized by man himself for various social reasons. "It is possible that, given the historical nature of human societies, we are victim to the needs of earlier social orders." For earlier societies, it may not have been a matter of severely *constraining* a powerful sexual impulse in order to maintain social stability; rather, it may have been a need to *invent* an importance for sexuality—not only to ensure high levels of reproductive activity, but also to provide a "socially available reward." And this reward could be used to achieve social order in a variety of ways. "A part of the legacy of Freud is that we have all become relatively adept at seeking out the sexual ingredient in many forms of nonsexual behavior."

We do not know for certain what our "sexual nature" is. Every society strongly directs its members and educates its young to a particular

If you don't tell them they'll find out about sex somehow. Many of the pitfalls of teenage sex could be avoided if parents could only talk frankly to their children about sex.

sexual nature, which serves that society's social order. Because our society is so diverse, it does not promote one set of sexual values and accords more importance to the individual, and to his development, than primitive societies have done.

Today's child has a great variety of life-styles open to him, and a great many confusing choices to make. On one hand, we protect him from contact of any kind with real bodies, real sexual relationships, and at the same time feed him with highly colored photographic fantasy. Compared with the sexual training of a primitive child, the sex education of a child in modern industrialized society is complicated and contradictory.

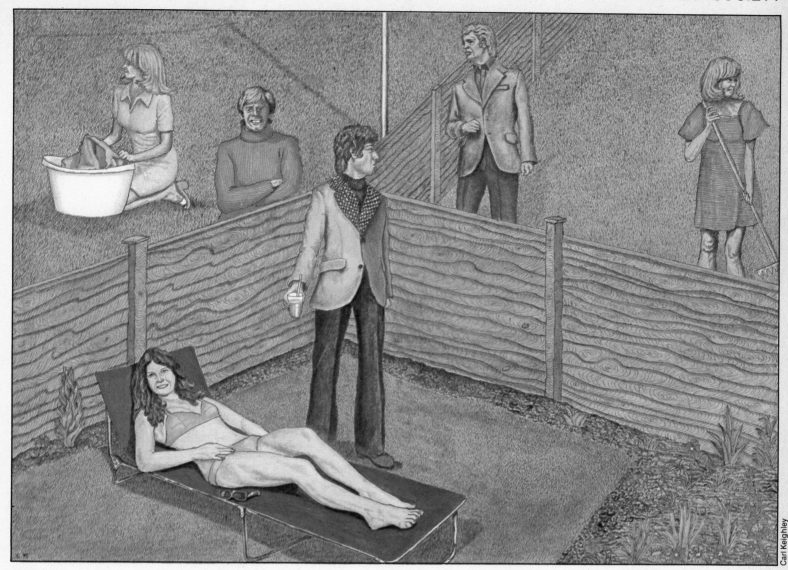

Carl Keighley

Pastures new

The other man's grass is always greener—and his wife is usually sexier too.

The desire to explore is part of man's nature; it is this—along with his ability to think, reason, conceptualize and feel emotion—that distinguishes him from the rest of the animal kingdom. The lion, for instance, contrary to old beliefs, has no desire to stray off his territory provided he has a mate and sufficient food for his family.

Competitive Spirit

Man, on the other hand, continues to seek new pastures. If this were not so, entire populations would have remained isolated, ignorant of the existence of others; war would have been a rarity, and so would trade; and the entire structure of our civilization would have been different. As it is, in spite of our "nesting," consolidating instincts, we still continue to look ahead, or over our shoulders, where the grass, we are certain, *is* greener.

Though we may have beautiful homes ourselves, someone always seems to have a better one. Though we have delightful, intelligent children, the woman down the street seems to be the mother of an angelic genius. And though our own husband, wife, or lover suits us fine, there is often the lingering suspicion that somewhere there exists one who would make us even happier. As long as the thought remains a passing one, there is little harm in it, but when we find ourselves obsessed by comparisons the situation becomes dangerous.

Literature and the media are, to a large extent, responsible for our wist-fulness and bent for comparison. Most small children are fed on a literary diet which includes some fairy tales, be they the classics like "Cinderella" or modern versions on the same theme—the cousin who married a millionaire, the boy down the street who became a boxing champion, the girl your mother was at school with who is now a famous movie star. To want to be like these heroes is natural enough, but it is a stage we should grow out of, certainly by the time we are adults—and most of us do.

But the media do not help, particularly commercial advertising. We may for instance be quite happy with our looks, homes, life-style—but the advertisers work hard at creating a certain discontent, a desire to improve ourselves and our way of life. After all, if we accepted our lot without question much of the merchandise on the market now, especially so-called "luxury" goods, would not sell.

Nevertheless the majority of people keep some sense of proportion, and though they may dream of being the one girl singled out to accompany the virile, handsome pipe-smoking play-boy, or the man chosen for the way his hair shines and the irresistible smell of his after-shave, they do not translate idle daydreams into genuine striving. As always, however, there are a few men and women who constantly seek something better.

Unable to Keep Up

People in any form of show business are often heard to blame the failure of relationships on their sudden success, and it is easy to see why. Success *is* exhilarating, and when your fans prove how desirable you are it is understandable that you are tempted to believe their exalted opinion of you. The man who marries when he is an office clerk or delivery boy, and later metamorphoses into a pop star may feel it unfair that he should be saddled with one woman, when thousands—often prettier or younger—are clamoring for his attention. The show-biz marriage that fails because one partner can not keep up with the other's rise to fame is common.

One young actor who has achieved considerable acclaim explained how easily the rift developed. "When I first became 'noticed' I was living with a super bird. We were actually thinking of getting married. Then it all started to happen—reviews, film offers—everyone seemed to want to know me. Susie was a quiet girl, but she was delighted with what promised to be the start of some kind of fame. I suppose I just took her for granted. To begin with she always came to parties and things with me, never pushed herself forward as some girls would, knowing their man was in the limelight. Of course I was flattered by all the attention I got, and I certainly fell for some of the girls I met. They were a breed I had only ever read about before in flashy magazines—rich, pretty and downright brazen.

"The inevitable happened: I started staying out later and later, eating in

Coty (UK) Ltd

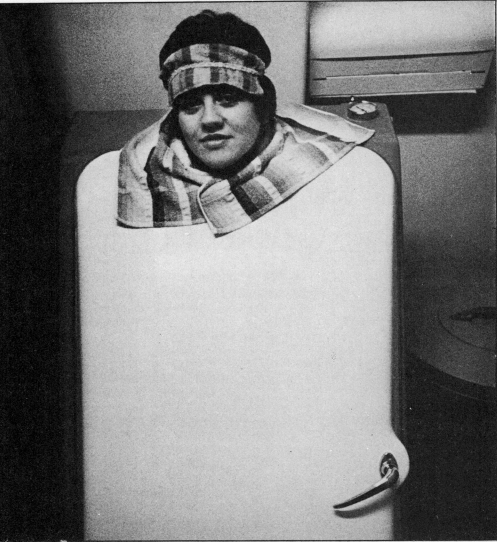

Another time, another place, another body, another face: if only she could escape from all this or emerge from those endless beauty treatments a new woman, her sex life would be much better.

Mark Edwards

2188

expensive restaurants, going to all the 'in' places, and Susie was with me less and less. You know, she never made a fuss, never blamed me. I did actually sleep around quite a bit, too —the first time I felt enormously guilty, but it got easier and I told myself it was all right, that Susie and I weren't married after all. Then I came home to our apartment—we had moved to a terrific one by then—after a two-day fling and found Susie gone. She left a note saying she still loved me and always would, but she knew she was a stone around my neck now and she didn't want to tie me down. It shows how arrogant I had become when I tell you I even felt a little annoyed that she should leave.

You Can't Turn Back the Pages

"It's easy to be wise now and see how stupid I was, but at the time I was very young and very bigheaded. I never found another girl like Susie. The ones I mixed with were like me—out for what they could get, always on the make. When all the fuss about me being the 'new' man died down, they didn't want to know me anymore. By this time, of course, I was used to being flattered, used to good living. I've had more 'success' since then, and I've lived with four different birds, but they never last.

"About six months ago I had this awful moment of truth when I knew, without being nostalgic, that Susie was the best thing that ever happened to me and that I would never find anyone better. I tried to trace her then. She had gone to Australia months before and I know I will never find her now, and I guess I don't deserve to. I might know she was my 'ideal', but though I'm older and you could say wiser, I'm still a selfish bastard and if she ever did reappear I would still behave in the way I did.''

A well-known radio personality, twenty years older than this young actor, reinforced the view that once the change of life-style has taken place, it is almost impossible to go back to a previous one. "I have been married three times. I don't think I'm either foolish or unpleasant, but like many people in television and radio— those who have made it I mean—I find it hard to feel the property of just one person. It may sound a cliché, but I belong far more to my public because, like it or not, I am 'known' to thousands; they are my job, and because the job is exacting, they are my life as well. Each of my wives has been a really nice person—it's me that's to blame.''

Whether we identify with it or not, it is not difficult to appreciate that such a man or woman (or, in fact, any celebrity) is more prone to indulge in "greener grass" speculation. But it also happens to people suffering from no such pressures. A psychiatrist explained that in many cases it has to do with a person's inability to deal with the reality of any given situation.

"Some of us, thank goodness only relatively few, are totally unable to live in the present, to recognize a situation for what it is. It is, of course, perfectly normal and healthy to employ fantasy from time to time. To cry for the moon occasionally is something we all do, but if we truly believe we can get it, there is something amiss with our psychological make-up. It would be facile to say that all men and women who have been married more than twice are guilty of infantile, or unreasoning attitudes to life and what a partnership implies, but I have certainly seen a number of people who fit that description.

"One woman in particular I remember. She was referred to me because she was obsessed with the desire to have plastic surgery. She wanted a face-lift, mammoplasty (surgery on the breasts), and her nose reshaped. In fact she was a good-looking woman of 42 with a body that any other woman of her age would have been glad to possess. She was in her third marriage and she thought it was in danger. Her sole reason for believing this was some inkling that her husband might prefer younger girls, and if she could have her appearance fixed she felt she would be able to compete.

Over The Hill

"Subsequent talks revealed that she had a history of wanting something better than what she had at the time: men, jobs, home, looks. She truly believed that the grass was greener over the hill, even though an observer would have said that her own couldn't be better. She had been an over-indulged child with wealthy parents who refused her nothing. In addition, her father had worshiped her and thought no man good enough for his only daughter. And her mother had constantly told her that there was nothing in this life you couldn't get if you wanted it badly enough.

"Another girl in a similar situation might have reacted in quite a different way, but she had taken her parents' assessment of her unquestioningly. So now approaching middle age, with two broken marriages behind her and a history of disappointments, she was

looking for another magical solution, still believing that change was the way to improvement.

"Unfortunately, though she was in many ways an intelligent woman, I was unable to guide her to a new assessment of herself, and she left my office in a huff one day, telling me I didn't understand her, and proving my point conclusively by saying she was going to another psychiatrist whom a friend had told her 'would work wonders'.

"She may be an extreme case, but in not being able to face up to her situation she has quite a few companions. Many of us run away from reality, and the ways we escape differ enormously. But believing it is our circumstances that are at fault and not ourselves is a fairly common condition, though it becomes serious when it is an unshakeable belief.''

Keeping Up with the Joneses

Many of us have to suffer comparison, sometimes unfavorable, from time to time. The housebound wife with limited funds, two or three children, and a husband who spends five days a week away from home is bound to wonder whether, given a wealthier husband, she might not still be as glamorous as the models she looks at in her weekly magazine. And her husband could be forgiven for occasionally wishing that he had a female companion as cool and sophisticated as his boss's personal assistant. But it is an immature man or woman who does not realize that even with more money to spend, there would still be grass that looked greener somewhere else.

One young wife almost lost her husband because he was prey to this kind of longing all the time. "No matter how pretty I made myself, or how good the meal I had prepared for our friends, he always managed to suggest that some other woman would have done better. He really was a classic case of someone trying to keep up with the Joneses. One woman in particular he seemed to admire above everyone else. She was married to one of his colleagues—always looked immaculate, kept a beautiful home, and seemed unable to do any wrong, at least in my husband's eyes. There were times when I could have torn her hair out, though she was always perfectly charming to me.

"At first I tried to keep up, to always be as good as her, but then after awhile my resentment took hold of me and I began to let everything go—my looks, the house, even the children suffered from lack of attention. If he had upped and left me at this point, an outside observer would have said he had every reason to. My mother put me on the right track again though, thank goodness. She could see what I was doing and she sympathized but told me I was doing it all wrong, and *would* lose him if I carried on in this way. She helped me get the house and the children back into shape again and insisted I buy some new clothes, get my hair done and generally pretty myself up. Then she enlisted the help of one of her younger friends. He started paying a lot of attention to me—at dinner parties he would not take his eyes off me, and kept telling my husband what a lucky dog he was to have a wife like me. Then I started to be out sometimes when my husband expected me to be home and would rush in looking flustered, but happy.

Constant Comparison

"It could all have gone hideously wrong, as such games can, but thankfully the ploy worked. My husband became quite violently jealous and finally insisted we talk about my 'affair'. I didn't actually deny that I was very flattered by all the attention I was getting, but implied it hadn't *yet* gone too far. I told him the truth then about the fact that I was fed up with constant comparison and had decided that I too was due for some admira-

tion. I think he was pretty chastened by the whole thing. Anyway, he stopped raving about his friend's wife. For awhile we cut down on entertaining, even though we both enjoyed having people to dinner or to play cards, and when we started being sociable I did see a difference in his behavior.

"Once or twice he would be on the point of suggesting that some other woman was superb, but he usually stopped before his praise got out of hand; we even laughed together as he was doing it. Part of his trouble is that he does have very high standards in everything. His parents brought him up to believe that your best is never good enough, and I think they are largely to blame for his constant striving towards perfection. I think we have our marriage pretty steady again now, but we would have failed if I hadn't worked very hard to make him see that the grass just isn't greener next door."

Sadly, however, it sometimes is. If a relationship is really threatened because one or both partners are immutably dissatisfied with the situation, then inevitably another man or woman may seem, and actually be, far more attractive. If love and physical attraction are dead, or irreversibly on the wane, then longing for someone else, be he real or imaginary, becomes part of the cause of the final breakup. One 30-year-old woman—whose marriage

had been "dead" two years before she finally made a move—put it like this: "At first you think it only might be greener over there but after awhile you *know* it is. Mine was the typical case of the out-of-love wife who transfers all her longings and aspirations onto one particular man. In my case he was totally unsuitable, as everyone except me could see. But he served a useful purpose in helping me to finally quit an outworn marriage. He was a schoolteacher and married to someone else—unhappily I thought, but only because I wanted it to be. He was tall, thickset, and quiet with huge brown eyes and a habit of staring at people in a way that made your stomach turn over. What I took to be veiled lust was in fact pure cogitation, but then I wanted to see love there. I bored everyone rigid with my infatuation, mostly because I endowed him with such godlike qualities.

A Shrewd Move

"I left my husband and moved so that I could see him every day going to and from school. I think, looking back, that he did genuinely like me, maybe desired me a little even, but he certainly wasn't in love with me, as he finally explained in a way that even I could understand. It took me a year to get over the pain of not being able to live with him in the paradise I had built up in my mind, but one day I realized that I still had a lot of life to look forward to and was only wasting time wishing I could be with him. I am married again now, and happily, but I would never knock the person who tells you that they yearn to be somewhere else, or with someone else, if they truly mean it. It was only by imagining that the grass *was* greener that I managed to get out of a relationship that was as dead as straw."

A psychiatrist would probably say that this woman did know the difference between dreaming and reality, that her longing for something better than she had was healthy because what she had was not good enough. But it is only by knowing how to differentiate between a pipe dream—an escape into fantasy that happens because you cannot deal with the present reality—and a true need to improve your lot that you can find out whether the grass is really greener over there, or whether it just appears so because your eyes are out of focus.

Keystone

The main attraction of the pop star is his unattainability. Most fans would be struck dumb if they met their idol, face to face.

interests, even in deference to the needs of the world as a whole.

We can well understand how the wealthier countries might inspire fierce resentment in the poorer over-populated nations in the grips of famine and drought, suffering widespread starvation and undernourishment. They do not take kindly to pressure to curb their numbers when it comes from nations which comprise only a third of the total population but consume 75 percent of the world's resources. If anything, they say their problem is not having *enough* people to develop their economies to bring their standards of living into line with those of the industrialized societies.

Smaller Families

Their preference for economic growth as opposed to population control is born of the fact that it promises quicker results. The various deprivations of their peoples call for immediate measures, while the objective of reducing the birthrate would take generations to achieve. Reinforcing this view is the disappointing record of government-sponsored family

planning programs. But there is no reason why these two approaches to the problem should be mutually exclusive. The conference was told by John D. Rockefeller III, a staunch advocate of family planning, that population control programs only work within a context which makes couples *want* to have small families.

That social context already exists in the highly developed industrialized countries. Here the desire to have fewer children is nurtured, and the provision of family planning services on a large scale makes it possible. The nations where the growth rate has fallen most dramatically are those where these services have been combined with rapid rises in agricultural modernization, industrial growth, and urban expansion. The inclination towards smaller families is a natural and beneficial spin-off.

Family size is not so much a matter of choice as of social tradition and cultural habit. These are not easily abandoned and can be transformed only gradually. A new social environment, such as comes with industrialization, can be created long before

people's ideas and attitudes have adjusted to it. The migration of rural families into the cities of a developing country is not going to change their breeding habits significantly. But immigrants from countries with traditions for large families have scaled down their families within one generation to a size acceptable to their host nation.

Planned Parenthood

What is it then about developed societies which favor a reduction in family size? For a start, birth control services are readily available, and contraception does not, by and large, infringe upon traditional or religious taboos. Admittedly the Roman Catholic church, with its worldwide influence, has yet to be persuaded—but on the whole family planning is socially and politically reinforced. The "new morality" allows for people to have as many children as they can provide for.

But the actual effectiveness of contraception as a means of population control has not gone unchallenged. It allows people to have as many children as they want, which is not the

Camera Press

same thing as the number which is socially desirable. By offering only the means for *individual couples* to control fertility, family planning neglects the means for *societies* to do so. But there are fewer parents in developed societies who *plan* large families.

National Preoccupation

The emancipation of women is one reason for this. Better education and increasing employment opportunities offer them a whole new range of positive interests which many consider preferable to a life of regular childbirth and interminable child rearing. And increased leisure time and a higher income make room for entertainment and recreational pursuits. A surfeit of children is time-consuming; it restricts mobility and eats into the family budget.

In materialistic societies, where "keeping up with the Joneses" is the national preoccupation, the pressure is on to maintain a high standard of living. With a fixed family income each extra child contributes to a decline of that standard, as parents find they can afford less and less. Furthermore they feel greater responsibility to-

wards their children, wanting to give them material advantages, education and recreational amenities. The more children there are to a family the more they have to forego luxuries in order to meet needs. In an economy of rising expectations people are being urged to want more for themselves and their children: advertisers remind them of the things they can have, which, in a family stretching its resources to the limit, have to be sacrificed.

Contrast this with the situation of a poorer population in a developing country. Where the activities of children are one of the few pleasures in life, reducing the family size is not so easy when there are no positive or apparent advantages in doing so. This is one, but not the main, reason why population control programs in poorer communities have not been particularly successful.

The primary obstacles to the successful introduction of family planning are ignorance and superstition. This was certainly so in India where the birthrate was reaching a crisis point that called for government action in the early 1950s. Sex education, contraceptives and vasectomy operations

Commuters in Tokyo would rather be crushed to death than late for work.

were made available. Inducements to take advantage of them were offered. Such a comprehensive scheme was easy to administer and, considering what was at stake, relatively cheap.

Financial Reward

But the program met with suspicion. Rumors circulated about the physical ill effects of contraception. It was put about that some methods caused cancer, some locked couples together, and others caused excessive bleeding. The apathy towards the government's initiative was increased by religious scruples and moral doubts. Financial reward for volunteering for contraceptive treatment or sterilization did not produce the expected results. Some women took out their intrauterine devices so that they could collect the bounty for having them fitted once again. The result is that the population in India, now standing at about 600 million, continues to edge upwards, probably reaching 717 million by 1980 and 808 million in the following five years.

Camera Press

The appeal of family planning depends very much on the type of community in which it is being introduced. For instance, in some territories of Kenya the demand for fertility clinics is greater than for birth control clinics. This is partly because the infant mortality rate is still high, but mainly because each birth provides another pair of hands, which can contribute more to the family income than it takes from it. Where this is still the case parents have a strong motive for not cooperating with a population policy.

Primitive agricultural economies still show a net gain from increasing the labor force; industrial economies with their emphasis on mechanization and automation do not. The transition from one to the other produces a surplus of labor and creates a situation in which children become a drain on family resources. The process of industrial development sets off a chain reaction: agricultural modernization reduces the need for a vast rural labor force; industry lures people out of rural areas into cities to earn their living. But technology demands skilled and semiskilled workers rather

than unskilled labor, and factories and offices need a higher proportion of administrative and clerical staffs. This increases the demand for education, which many people see as the key to a real population solution. Education takes children out of the labor force so that they no longer contribute to the family income. These children, who might once have been an economic advantage, are now a liability, and the motive for family planning is established.

Mixed Blessing

It is therefore clear that economic development and industrial expansion are not just a means of providing for large numbers but actually a means of reducing them. They also offer a way to exploit resources. Industrial advance therefore seems to be the solution to both the problem of "too many people" and that of "not enough to go around." But this is questionable. It is naive to suppose that resources of food, materials and energy are themselves unlimited and that it is only lack of equipment and know-how which stops them from being sufficiently tapped.

Farm workers in South Africa are paid wages below starvation level.

Technology is a mixed blessing, a treacherous friend. Its purpose is to increase the yield of natural resources and to decrease the workload of man. But in doing so, it uses up more resources than any population, so in order to justify itself it has to increase productivity correspondingly beyond the demands of an expanding population—a vicious circle.

Some thirty years ago the visionary futurologist Buckminster Fuller estimated that the average American had the technological equivalent of 150 slaves working for him. Now these human substitutes number 400, which, in terms of strain on resources, is like having 400 extra mechanical mouths to feed. Unless technology can guarantee to provide itself with a reasonable standard of upkeep, it will have defeated its own purpose.

Technology reaches beyond city boundaries and into the fields: the modernization of agriculture brings with it the fear that artificial stimulants to the land—chemical fertilizers and pesticides—may in the long run inhibit output by interfering with the time-honored cycles of nature. Meanwhile industry—and the cities in which it flourishes—contributes to the deterioration of the environment by disgorging waste and pollutants into the land, into coastal and inland waters and into the atmosphere. In short, unless industry and technology can support themselves, and over-compensate for their own deleterious by-products, they will cease to pay their way, cease to be the servant of the population. And even if they can support themselves, they also have to allow for both the rapid depletion of resources and the greater demands of a rising population.

In poorer nations, with vast populations, labor is the most abundant resource: any reduction of the human workload as a result of technological advance can often make the situation worse. Assuming that technology can find all the food the people need, their most pressing demand is for jobs to produce incomes for their families. What is needed here, according to one economist, Dr. E. F. Schumacher, is not "high technology," but "intermediate technology"—a system which utilizes the excess manpower, keeps pace with the population's technical expertise, and enables people to make the best use of their own natural resources. His message to the developing nations is "think small." This scaling down of operations to fit the real capacity of individual nations will ultimately increase productivity and profit, will avoid wastage, reduce pollution, provide full employment, and raise the standard of living. It will also redress the imbalance between the demands of huge populations and the exploitation of the environment. The accepted answer to the population problem—in economic terms—has shifted in the last few years from "proceed at all costs" to "proceed with caution."

Inalienable Right

There is a wide measure of agreement on this line of thought, but it is not easy to put into practice. The Bucharest conference was at least an indication that we are finally aware of our danger. The experts are unanimously worried about the state of our planet, but few are without hope. However, if their advice and warnings go completely unheeded, we must either expect the worst or be prepared to reduce our consumption and curb our population.

To have children is an inalienable human right. Family size is a personal matter, so any attempts to reduce numbers by force of law would be regarded as a gross infringement of individual liberty. But even that seems preferable to some of the "natural" ways in which populations throughout history have been periodically cut down: war, famine, disease, and, to a lesser degree, accident, which wipe out whole segments of any population. War and disease are often the result of overpopulation, and while drought, famine, natural disasters such as floods and earthquakes, and

Famine is one of nature's ways of cutting down the world's population.

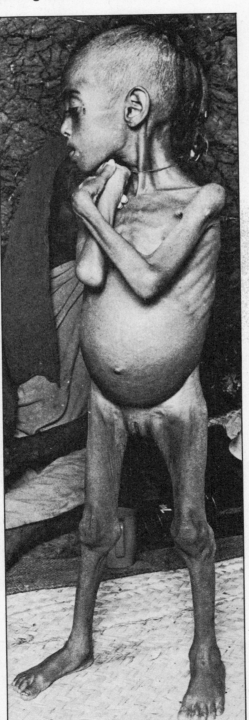

Camera Press

other "acts of God" are not related to population size, they often occur in the most thickly populated areas.

War reduces populations by more than just the "death toll" (which the two world wars of recent history brought to unprecedented levels). As the majority of casualties are young fighting men who, if they survived, would father children, the loss is more significantly felt in the following generation. But postwar periods are often marked by an acceleration of growth as the nation consciously strives to restore its depleted population and regain its strength—often for yet another war. In more belligerent times it was a constant cause of anxiety to mothers that the sons they were producing were more "cannon fodder."

Question Mark

Diseases which assume epidemic proportions—cholera, yellow fever, malaria, smallpox—do not bring death on the same scale as they used to. During the 1930s, malaria was the cause of as many as half the deaths on the island of Ceylon (now Sri Lanka) but, when DDT was introduced in 1946 to bring the disease-carrying mosquitoes under control, the death-rate fell immediately. Since then the deathrate has halved and the birthrate has doubled. But the control of disease depends on medical treatment and supplies, and densely populated areas of poorer countries—the seedbeds of disease and infection—are the very places where medical services are likely to be inadequate.

No one likes to believe that the only solution to the population problem is a disaster of cataclysmic proportions: a global famine, an uncontrollable epidemic, or a nuclear holocaust. But we can be certain that, sooner or later, one or the other will occur if we continue to propagate with such abandon. Equally certain is that such a catastrophe can be avoided if we aim purposefully at a reduction of birthrate and equity in the sharing of resources. What is uncertain, however, is whether we are at all capable of being sensible, unselfish, restrained and global-minded.

A big question mark also hangs over the ability of science, technology, and medicine to come up with new resources and from these to create the "more" needed by future populations —or to make the "less" go farther. So far they have succeeded, but there is no reason to think that they will necessarily do so forever, and it is wisest not to bank on it.

Bob Harvey

Gift of the gab

We rely heavily on language as a means of communicating with our fellows, but we come unstuck when we want to talk to someone who doesn't speak the *same* language.

The Hebrews considered language to be a gift from God. Many other ancient races recognized that the uniqueness of human language separated us from the lower animals, and so decided that their own language had been handed to them a completely fashioned divine ability.

Tower of Babel

The Bible laid down that until God punished the race of man for his presumption in building the Tower of Babel, all men spoke the same God-given language. This was widely supposed to have been Hebrew, and King James IV of Scotland is said to have raised two children in isolation to test the hypothesis. They spoke in "very guid Ebrew," although we may suspect that King James' translators were not the best.

At other times in history, a number of similar attempts have been made: the Egyptian Pharaoh Psammitichos found that the first word spoken by his experimental subjects was the Phrygian word for "bread."

The study of language is very complex, encompassing a number of separate disciplines. Linguistics, psychology, sociology, anthropology, brain structure and function, and the anatomy of the vocal apparatus must all be taken into account in language study. This situation is made even more complex by disputes as to what actually constitutes a language.

Danish, Swedish, and Norwegian can be understood, to a large extent, by natives of any of these countries but are universally considered to be different languages. Local dialects, however, in a country as small as Italy can differ among each other far more than do the Scandinavian languages, yet they are still considered to be dialects of the "Italian" language.

With few exceptions, we find that a language does not suddenly cease to be heard beyond the limit of territory inhabited by its speakers. Language crosses national boundaries and merges imperceptibly into the one spoken by the adjacent peoples. Only in highly developed nations where all the inhabitants are exposed to a consistent radio or television language does a standard language emerge.

This has resulted in the disappearance or suppression of many local dialects, although in Britain, at least, the reverse tendency is now emerging. From the Greek and Roman empires to the modern day, a "rustic" accent was not socially acceptable in urban areas. Now, however, dialects are more acceptably renamed "regional accents," and are becoming a source of local pride.

It is agreed that language is a universal ability. Every race or national grouping has a spoken language (about 10,000 in all, plus an unknown number of extinct languages), and many have evolved a written language.

But how each person goes about learning his language is not completely understood. The group of language psychologists founded by Noam Chomsky has postulated that at certain stages of a child's mental development there exists a sort of "intellectual vacuum" in which part of the brain becomes available for language learning. This so-called rationalist school holds that the child has an innate tendency to produce language, and that experience of the environment has a minimal effect.

On the other hand, the influential behaviorist school of thought, founded by B. F. Skinner, holds that language, together with almost all other human abilities, must be learned as a result of experience of the environ-

ment. Experience will then determine all subsequent behavior.

Both groups agree that children need only limited exposure to spoken language during their development; this is sufficient to enable them to comprehend and learn effectively. Which school of thought is correct? As in so many similar disputes, the answer is both or neither.

Coo and Chuckle

There is much evidence to confirm the rationalist view, that the tendency to develop language is built into the brain, but the theory holds only for the acquisition of a spoken language, and many sophisticated races of the past have conducted their civilizations satisfactorily by means of a spoken language only. In these circumstances, a written language first comes into being as a reminder to help in commercial transactions, or as a record for taxation or religious purposes. Methods such as the knotted strings used by ancient South American Indians to convey messages are a simple form of mnemonic, or memory-jogging device. Pictographs, the pictorial symbols used by the ancient Egyptians, convey more complex ideas but still do not approach the true alphabets used today, where every letter conveys a specific sound.

In a human child, the first signs of speech, or attempts at speech, seem to appear spontaneously. By the age of four months, a normal child will be cooing and chuckling. At this age he can sit, supported by a pillow, and his neck muscles support his head firmly enough to allow him to view his environment. Significantly, the child's first vocal attempts are usually directed at its mother.

By six to nine months, the child almost instinctively produces a speech-like babble. He will mimic sounds which interest him and form simple words like "mama" and "dadda." This stage of spontaneous babbling is very important in the development of language and appears to reflect a child's innate ability to produce language, rather than his degree of learning. Children who are born deaf begin to babble at this age, but soon cease. It seems that the sound is produced automatically, but without the feedback normally obtained by

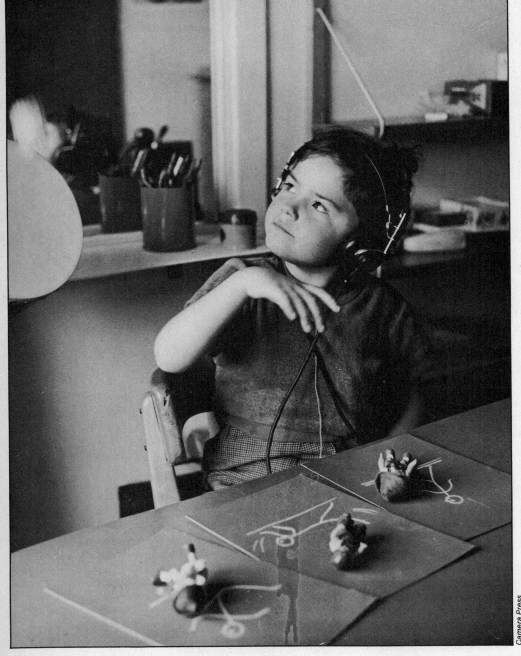

Camera Press

A three-year-old deaf girl is taught to speak at the Voldslokka Clinic in Norway. She is able to hear sounds on electro-acoustic earphones and is taught the meaning of the sounds by pictures and dolls.

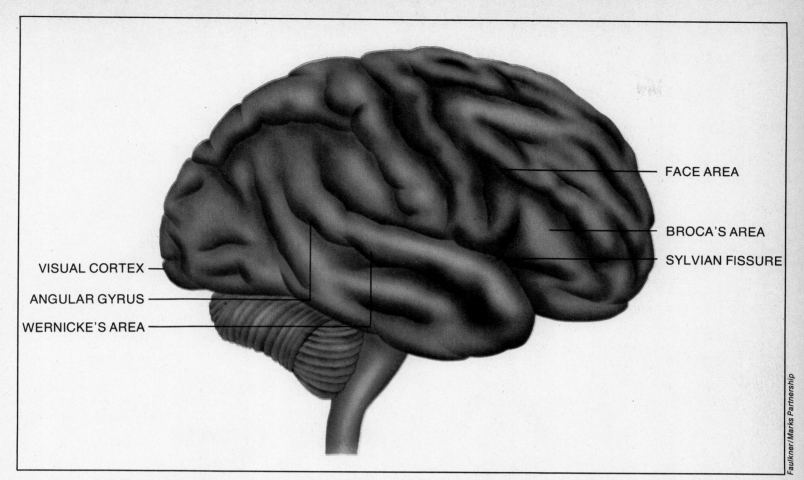

VISUAL CORTEX

ANGULAR GYRUS

WERNICKE'S AREA

FACE AREA

BROCA'S AREA

SYLVIAN FISSURE

Faulkner/Marks Partnership

hearing the responses of the mother or other individuals, the child is unable to refine his babblings into proper speech. This childlike chatter has been likened to a violinist tuning his instrument by comparison with notes produced by other instruments.

Largely Gibberish

One 14-month-old child was unable to make any sound for six months because of surgery on his throat. Immediately after his throat was repaired, he was able to make the general sounds (but not proper words) which were appropriate to his actual age, without ever going through the stage of babbling. His brain had evidently developed past the stage at which babble is generated.

At 12 to 18 months, the child knows a few simple words and can respond to some straightforward commands. By about 21 months, he should know around 200 words and will ask to be told appropriate names by pointing to objects and looking questioningly at an onlooker. He can now put together simple two-word phrases.

The biggest spurt in the child's language-learning ability comes at about two-and-a-half, when sentences are constructed, word order is established, and the child forms his own peculiar rules of grammar. By

three years, most children have a vocabulary of 1,000 words and are beginning to respond to generally accepted grammatical rules, rather than their own constructions.

This sequence holds for all languages, however complex, but the timetable varies enormously between individuals. Some children do not coo until six months. This does not mean that they are mentally retarded; however, since the age at which a child starts to coo and chuckle will coincide with the time he begins to support his head without letting it flop back, his mental development at this age is closely tied to his physical development. His ability to produce "language" does not appear to be closely tied to the amount of practice he has had, although in an impoverished environment, where the child is never able to copy adult speech, his own language is liable to be largely gibberish.

The part played by auditory feedback, or hearing our own voices, is critical, supported by the deaf child who never progresses beyond the babbling stage. Auditory feedback is continuously used to monitor our speech, and whenever this is interrupted, speech disturbances may occur. When an adult who has learned to speak fluently becomes deaf, the

Language areas of the brain are thought to be on the left side. If Broca's area is damaged, speech is affected; if Wernicke's area is damaged, comprehension is lost.

quality of his speech rapidly deteriorates, unless special training is undertaken, because this feedback is no longer received.

If speech is played back through earphones after a momentary delay of about 0.2 seconds, the rate of speaking first slows, then may deteriorate into stuttering. By modifying the input so that the auditory feedback is concentrated in one ear or the other, it can be demonstrated that sounds presented to the right ear have greater effect on speech. The input from the right ear is channeled to the left side of the brain, and this confirms the view which has long been held, that the language center of the human brain is situated in the left hemisphere.

Brain Damage

Until this simple demonstration had been devised, it was possible to study the part played by the brain in language behavior only under unnatural conditions—during brain surgery, by observing the behavior of people with brain damage, or by postmortem examination of the brain. Through

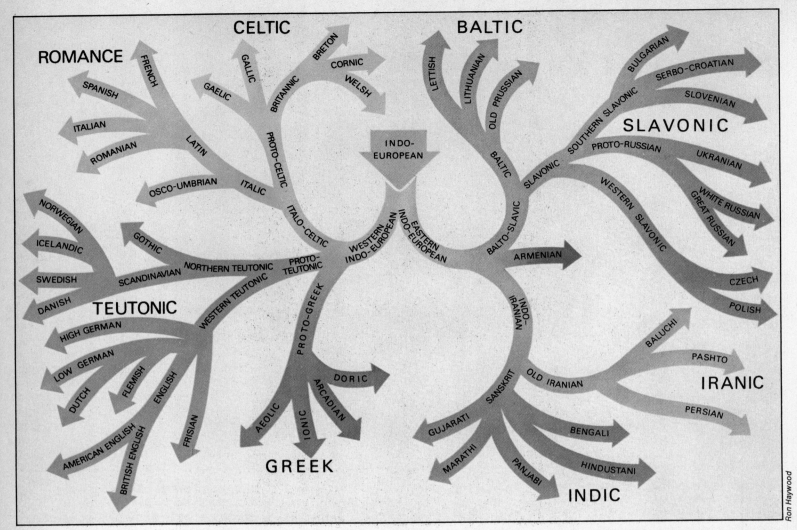

ROMANCE · CELTIC · BALTIC · SLAVONIC · TEUTONIC · GREEK · INDIC · IRANIC

Ron Haywood

study of the brain under these conditions, as well as study of various types of language disorders, particular areas of the brain associated with the ability to understand and reproduce language have been identified.

One of the commonest language disorders is aphasia, a loss or impairment of the ability to use words which usually results from rupture of blood vessels in the brain. In 1861, Paul Broca, a French scientist, pointed out the correlation between aphasia and damage to a specific part of the left side of the brain (subsequently called Broca's area). This "language" area lies just in *front* of the part of the cortex controlling the muscles of the face, tongue, and palate—those responsible for producing speech.

Verbal Shorthand

In Broca's aphasia, speech becomes very slow and words are abbreviated into a sort of verbal shorthand. Sufferers reply to questions with poorly articulated phrases or often merely with a single word. It might be supposed that aphasia is simply muscular paralysis resulting from damage to this region. But facial muscles, un-

like the language facilities controlled by Broca's area, can be controlled quite effectively by the *other* half of the brain. Damage to this area results in weakness in the facial muscles.

Broca soon discovered that damage to the corresponding "language" area on the right side of the brain did not affect language ability. This is an example of cerebral dominance, where one side of the brain effectively takes over a particular function. Subsequent work has shown that 97 percent of brain-damaged patients with permanent language defects have sustained injury to the left side.

Damage to Broca's area results in slow and incomplete speech, but it was found that damage in other areas could produce quite different types of speech disorder. In 1874, Carl Wernicke found that damage to an area farther towards the back of the brain, on the left side, caused a rapid and sometimes incoherent babble. Wernicke's aphasia results in speech which, superficially, sounds perfectly fluent, with apparently normal grammar and rhythm. But when the content of this speech is examined it is found to be almost meaningless. The

Many of the world's major languages developed over a period of 5,000 years from Indo-European roots.

sufferer talks quite readily about nothing in particular and may drop totally inappropriate words into his conversation ("I drove to work in my table"). Even more disconcertingly, he coins neologisms, inventing a new and meaningless word. Another difference between these two basic types of aphasia is that where damage to Broca's area does not affect comprehension of language, in Wernicke's aphasia the sufferer may no longer understand language.

Roses Are Red

With Wernicke's aphasia, the sufferer can no longer comprehend either spoken or written language and will be unable to reproduce these forms of communication correctly. Conversely, when Broca's area is damaged, the patient retains full understanding but is unable to articulate his messages. Apparently, comprehension of language is accomplished in Wernicke's area, and communication via the vocal appara-

2204

tus is actually effected by Broca's area. This implies that the two areas are connected, and other forms of aphasia resulting from damage to the connections can be predicted.

Such forms of aphasia do occur, and they cast more light on the function of the brain in producing language. In one study, a woman remained completely comatose for nine years, after suffering from carbon monoxide poisoning. During that time, she never spoke spontaneously but could complete phrases spoken by others. If she heard, ''Roses are red,'' she would repeat the phrase and complete it: ''Roses are red, violets are blue, sugar is sweet, and so are you.'' If a song was played to her, she would eventually sing along with the music, and finally would sing the entire song unaccompanied after having been cued in by the first few bars.

Flash Cards

After her death, brain examination showed a most unusual injury which isolated her speech center from the rest of her cortex. But it did not seem to matter to the type of speech she could produce. Both Broca's and Wernicke's areas remained intact, and these turn out to be ''switching stations'' of a sort. Apparently, Wernicke's area recognized the chant and Broca's area took it up automatically: she could repeat speech independently of the areas of the brain which initiate original speech. The brain appears to treat poetry and singing—both measured and semiautomatic verbal expression—as something quite separate from actual language, as in all these types of aphasia comprehension of song seems to be normal.

In some patients, damage to other brain areas results in specific forms of aphasia: alexia and agraphia—the loss of ability to read and write—while full comprehension and use of spoken language is retained. They are in the anomalous position of understanding a word when it is spoken to them, but not when it is spelled out. That is, they recognize the word as a complete sound, rather than as a collection of separate symbols and sounds. This child can learn to ''read'' by identifying individual words visually, in the form of the ''flash cards'' often used in primary schools. In this form of teaching, the child has no idea of the alphabet, or of the sounds portrayed by each letter, but merely recognizes the word by its visual shape. The individual sounds are learned much later. The loss of the ability to read and write results from a separation of the visual and auditory language areas, which produces a superficial resemblance to the language learning ability of a young child. Dyslexia, which is a congenital difficulty in reading unrelated to intelligence, may also be associated with a disturbance in the neural pathways connecting the language ability parts of the brain.

As the child's brain develops, the complexity of the connections between nerve cells in the cortex increases, and with it the ability to comprehend more of the hidden structure of language. Children aged five to six usually assume that any person or object named in a sentence is taking an active part in the subject being discussed. For example, when children were presented with sentences like ''The wolf is happy to bite,'' or ''The duck is fun to bite,'' and asked to explain which of the two animals involved was actually biting, they thought both wolf and duck were biting. But around six to six and a half years of age they begin to comprehend the deeper structure of the sentence, but by no means reliably. By age ten the normal child can comprehend all such sentences.

Wind Instrument

The human vocal apparatus is capable of producing only a limited number of sounds, although these can be given distinctive treatment by different national groupings. All vocal sounds are produced in the same way, by liberating air compressed in the lungs. As we exhale, air is forced past the vocal cords in the larynx. These are a pair of flaplike membranes stretched across the larynx, which can be tensed by small muscles. The vocal cords vibrate like the reed in a wind instrument.

Varying the muscles' tension produces higher or lower notes, but producing the characteristic sounds of speech is more complex. The lips, tongue, and the soft palate at the back of the throat can all move to produce a characteristic sound. Interruption of the air streams or a sudden release of pressure can produce ''hard'' sounds, such as t, p, or the ''hard'' sound of ch. When the soft palate diverts air through the nasal passages, the English m or n is produced. Apart from the characteristic forms of the English language, there are a number of more unusual sounds, such as the guttural rs of German, the trilled rs found in French, and the clicks found in some African languages, which are almost impossible for a European or American to reproduce.

In describing a language, it may be broken down into simple sounds, or phonemes. These are the minimal recognizable component sounds of a word, but do not necessarily represent a single letter (for example, th in English). In a perfect alphabet, each phoneme could be represented by a different letter. The nearest to this ideal situation are the Welsh and the Finnish languages, while the worst is probably the English language.

Detective Work

Local dialects result when the phonemes in a word vary slightly in pronunciation. Then the change is usually consistent through a number of other words. There is an almost imperceptible but continuous change from dialect to a distinct language, as permanent and distinctive pronunciation shifts occur. These can often be traced back to some ancient people who left their linguistic mark on the areas they once inhabited.

The largest language family of all is the Indo-European group from which many of the world's major languages are descended. By complicated detective work, tracing shifts in phonemes and words over long periods of time, linguists can make close guesses at the original Indo-European words which give rise to their modern successors. The word ''father'' has many related variants: pita (Sanskrit, an ancient Indian language), pater (Greek and Latin), and fadar (Gothic). These four words are all obviously related, but there has been a change from the p sound to f in languages which are known to be recent. So it is probable that the original word began with p, or a sound like it.

Recent languages which have evolved naturally are Pidgin English and Creole French; both are complex mixtures of other languages, superimposed on a very simple framework of native words. They have gradually become established as true languages in their own right, but still have a haunting familiarity to speakers of some of the original tongues. ''Mi gat trifela buk'' is Melanesian Pidgin English for ''I have three books.'' These languages are a direct outgrowth of colonization in the eighteenth and nineteenth centuries and the resulting need to provide easy communication between the colonizers and colonized. As such, they reflect the basic function of all languages: to communicate with others as naturally and spontaneously as possible within a mutually recognizable system.

Three's a crowd

Some men can't do anything without their buddy, and when the best man goes on the honeymoon too it's time to part the pals. We all need friends, but the guy who's wedded to his cronies is no hot tip in the marriage stakes. If love is to survive, sidekicks must be kicked aside.

Friendship can mean more than love. A marital relationship built around amity and a comfortable sexual tie may easily outlast the white-hot romance that conceals basic incompatibility. And, over the years, companionship can come to seem more valuable than sexual fervor.

Friendships outside the marriage, too, can help to stabilize the relationship and provide support for the couple at moments when they find it difficult to communicate. But there can be a dark side to the coin when friendship interferes with a couple's life together—even drives them apart.

Not Enough

Friendship between a man and a woman can cement them together for the wrong reasons and become a time bomb threatening to blow apart an apparently amicable relationship because the two people are confused about the nature of their desires.

A lonely boy and girl meet and find they enjoy sharing activities, knowing they will have each other's company where before they were solitary. Perhaps love dawns—perhaps it does not. But they drift into marriage because neither can face the future alone.

Life may be very pleasant, but friendship is not love, so the niggly problems of living together and the resulting emotional quarrels that lovers indulge in and overcome may cause resentments to build beneath the tranquil facade. Instead of sharing, the partners may begin to exploit each other as their original friendship crumbles under the strain of day-to-day living. Eventually one, possibly the one who feels most frightened of loneliness, becomes an emotional appendage of the other.

"When I met Georgia," said John, "I didn't know any other women at all —my time went on hobbies which I shared with a few other guys. Georgia was a cousin of one of the guys who'd just moved into town. We found we shared an interest in hypnotism, tarot cards and that kind of thing. We'd spend hours up in my room talking —I even hypnotized Georgia—and eventually we ended up in bed.

"The silly thing was just how little it meant to us—for me it was partially curiosity to see what Georgia's body looked like, and years later she told me that it had been a favor on her part which she thought I'd like. But we got ourselves caught on an escalator of expectations. Because we were making love we felt we had to tell each other we were in love.

"But once we were married, what was the point? We couldn't spend all day reading each other's cards. Neither of us wanted children and we didn't really want the responsibility of buying a house and so on. After a while we virtually made a pact to play at marriage—it was more like sharing an apartment with a friend of the opposite sex. On that level we'd have

Dave Smith

been fine, but the problem, of course, was that we were committed to each other in all sorts of ways—sharing a bed each night, for example. There were times when I resented Georgia intensely because she made it clear she wanted me to stimulate her physically. I sort of liked our being in bed together, being cozy, but I'd just lost interest in the idea of a sexual relationship with her.

"Curiously enough, we were both widening our contacts with others. I was getting to know Georgia's girl-friends, she was spending time with my pals. It's something that should have happened *before* we contemplated marriage. Eventually we decided to separate and our divorce is through now. We're still friendly—but we've both learned that we're looking for more than that."

Friendship can seduce two people into an unsuccessful marriage; when turned outside the relationship it can also bring another possibility of breakdown. Jealousy is the basic danger. Although psychologists know that the partners in a successful marriage are likely to have more friends—both in common and separately—than the partners in a rocky relationship, it is exactly those whose marriage could benefit from an open attitude who fear the threat of friendship.

Escape Clause

Sometimes this jealousy is sexual—a man or woman, unsure of his or her partner's affections, may be disturbed by the idea of a friendship with someone of the opposite sex. Even if the friendship is, in fact, based on non-sexual attraction, it can produce strains in a marriage just because the insecure partner is unable to accept its platonic basis. In this view, all male-female relationships lead to sex, and a married man or woman must give up any idea of a nonsexual friendship. And when a marriage is precariously based, uncertainties in the relationship between husband, wife and friend generate tensions that can themselves lead to awareness of the sexual possibilities outside marriage.

Resentment often builds, however, against the time and emotional effort expended on friends whether of the same or the opposite sex, rather than against a possible sexual involvement. Sometimes this time and effort really is excessive. In other situations the resentment stems more from a false idea of marriage as an all-exclusive partnership; one partner makes such neurotic and compulsive demands for love that they prevent

Marshall Cavendish

the other partner from entering any external relationships. In both cases the marriage comes under strain.

A man or woman may use friendships as an excuse for evading a full commitment to marriage. Drifting off to spend an occasional evening with the boys, giving up a few hours to advise a friend on personal problems, or helping a girlfriend with a tricky piece of dressmaking may be reasonable activities in themselves, but when they begin happening every evening and Saturdays and Sundays too it suggests something is wrong.

Talking over marital problems with a friend may be seen as a betrayal of trust by the marriage partner.

Taking refuge in these undemanding pastimes—and compared to making a marriage work this is what they are, however much effort the person concerned claims to be putting in—reveals the urge to act as though the marriage does not exist as a binding emotional relationship.

The man who appears wedded to his cronies or the woman who spends all her time with her canasta-playing friends may never have seen more in the marriage than a simple and socially acceptable guarantee of intermittent sexual release linked to a meal ticket or housekeeping arrangement. With such an arid relationship it is no wonder one or both partners look for more congenial outlets.

In other cases, escape into outside friendships is an immature reaction to the problems of marriage. A young man or woman may have grown used to a reasonably active social life without realizing how much of it depended on being part of a group of single people. When this apparently ceases with marriage—because conflicting wishes, household tasks, and caring for a baby intervene—there is a gap unfilled by a different kind of mutually enjoyable social life that takes into account the constraints of marriage. Sooner or later arises the temptation to fall back into the only kind of social round so far experienced—and this one-sided plunge exerts a divisive influence on the marriage.

Subtler pressures develop when friends are used as safety valves for the emotional pressures building within a marriage. A full partnership implies that the two people involved try to share and face up to their problems together—doing this may include seeking professional guidance or, at a less formal level, talking individually or together with friends. But some people step away from problems that they might be able to cope with if they faced up to them and substitute talking to friends for real action.

Like the Weather

Complaining about the wife's deficiencies over drinks in a bar or exposing a husband's failing at morning coffee is meaningless and can become embarrassing for all involved. If there are real difficulties, the only person worth talking to is the partner—for matters to improve, both partners probably have to change the way they behave towards each other and this cannot happen if they are not communicating. And revealing problems in the semi-public setting of a group of acquaintances reduces them to the status of an inevitable burden which can be lightened slightly by joking about it. Like the weather, they have to be accepted rather than dealt with.

"That Harry can be a real pain," said Randy. "Half a dozen of us used to meet for a couple of hours in a local bar after work on a Friday evening. You know how it goes—a few beers, chew the fat a little, some work problems maybe that could be sorted out,

since we're all in the same line. It's just a matter of relaxing a little in readiness for the weekend.

"Harry really threw me when he asked me to stay behind after the others left one Friday. He bought another round and we shifted over to a booth. He put his face real close to mine and said, 'What do you do when your wife's frigid?' 'Get yourself another broad,' I replied. 'No, no. I'm being serious. Peggy just isn't interested in making love. I can hammer away for hours and she doesn't react.'

"What can you say? I told him they ought to see a marriage counselor. There's no future in trying to give advice. It's crazy to say, 'Have you tried this, or that?' and anything else is sympathy which may or may not be helpful if it leaves things just like they are. Peggy, the couple of times I met her, was OK—pretty, not neurotic or anything. I'd have gotten in the sack with her myself if it was going to help."

Innocent Party

"We left it at that. But then a couple of months later Tony gave me a call. Harry had converted him—he really thought we ought to be in there laying on broads and lawyers for Harry, marriage manuals or something for Peggy. Tony's Eagle Scout mentality can run wild at times. Harry had been talking to all of us one by one until he found someone who'd go along with his conviction that Peggy was the wrong woman for him.

"That Friday night session quietly stopped happening. Drinking friends just aren't the same as an encounter group or marriage forum. We weren't geared up to handling a real problem—whatever it was that was going wrong in Harry's marriage."

Even if friends and acquaintances do interest themselves in each other's marital difficulties, this can be more dangerous than helpful. Closing ranks around one or other of the partners may reinforce the view that one is to blame for what is going on while the other is an innocent party. The reality is likely to be a confused mixture of sad failures. Advice given in these situations is likely to present a false stereotype of the nature of men and women and of marriage itself. Even people who themselves have satisfying and sincere relationships with others may still talk in a way that suggests all relationships depend on exploitation to some extent.

People are usually flattered to be asked for help and, sometimes, may become heavily involved in a situation which can only worsen as a result

of their meddling. Curiosity may impel an outsider to ask deep, searching questions about sexual and emotional aspects of the relationship, and a person in difficulty may find some cathartic release in revealing the most intimate secrets to a third party. A desire to tamper—linked to a false belief that it is possible to "impose" a happy solution on other people—may lead the confidant to map out a course of action that has little connection with the real needs of the couple.

A simplistic idea put forward by a forceful personality may persuade a vacillating husband or wife to do something he or she will later regret. Worse, suggesting that the "guilty" party requires a good talking to is but a short step from offering to do the job. However well known he is to both partners, an outsider taking on this kind of responsibility is treading on very dangerous ground. He is extremely likely to have a one-sided view of what is going on, and there is no guarantee that the "errant" partner will be interested in his opinions anyway. And most upsetting, as soon as the third party makes an active move, there is no disguising the fact that marital secrets have been bandied about. Whatever their view of the situation, there are few people who would not be upset to find that their partner has been discussing matters that they thought were private.

Advice may not be as disinterested as it sounds, either. A man hoping to have an affair with an abandoned wife may feed a husband's conviction that he should seek a separation. An older woman may compensate for a sense of failure in her own marriage by maliciously advising a young wife to take revenge on the whole of mankind.

Sidekick Syndrome

"Have an affair yourself," was Yvette's suggestion when Carole told her she thought Gerald was seeing another woman. "Men are after what they can get. Why shouldn't you enjoy yourself too? Get yourself proof that Gerald really does have a mistress and you'll have him exactly where you want him—under your thumb. That's the way I dealt with Philip." If Carole's dismayed anger at Gerald's suspected infidelity had persisted, she might well have taken Yvette's distorted advice and followed her into a loveless and unproductive relationship.

Same-sex friendships that drain vitality from a person's relationships can start well before marriage, and establish a pattern that interferes with the search for a partner and later with

Ron Embleton

Green-eyed monster

Jealousy hath a human face—say the Songs of Experience. Could it ever be yours?

There is a particularly painful emotion which affects all of us at one time or another. It is that variety of "psychic toothache" we call jealousy.

Jealousy can arise in many situations and if taken to extremes can prove a highly destructive force. Mrs. Jackson crossexamines her husband in a rather unsubtle way about his business trip. He becomes resentful and interrogates her again about *that time* when she returned so late from her friend's home and was given a lift by a man she met there. Four-year-old Sonya is angry and upset at the fuss the visitors make over her new sister and says that mummy loves the baby more than her. Teenage Joseph gets furious with his girlfriend for the smiles and attention she gives a handsome stranger at the dance. He sulks and shows interest in another girl.

All four of them are experiencing

that poignant, hurtful (and yet, at times, oddly enjoyable) blend of hostility, anxiety, envy and resentment which makes up jealousy. Anxiety and envy arise from the belief that your position in another's affection or esteem is being undermined, or from a feeling that someone is getting more than his fair share of available resources. The hostility and resentment come from the attempt to maintain a certain status. They make for a corrosive mixture. Yet jealousy, after all, is a motive which lies at the core of man's life as a social creature, though no society has ever tried to make a virtue of envy. It is an emotion or drive which occurs as soon as two individuals become capable of mutual comparison.

Jealousy (within certain limits) is a normal by-product of growing up. All children are susceptible to this emo-

tion and, despite parental efforts, it is impossible to banish it altogether. Its roots go so deep that certain forms of animal behavior can be viewed as envy-like activity: take the farmyard pecking order.

Brotherly Hate

The earliest jealousies, and perhaps the most agonizing ones, occur within the family. Jealousy between brothers and sisters—sibling rivalry—is almost inevitable: the Bible is a source of many case histories, the best known being the story of Cain and Abel. Although not many boys go so far as killing their brothers, the actions of Cain appear in the fantasies of many, and feelings similar to his can often be unraveled during psychotherapeutic sessions with children. Then there was Joseph, the favored son of Jacob, whom God had blessed with a dream of greatness. He was envied by his brothers. "And they conspired against him to slay him . . . and they took him, and cast him into a pit."

The Austrian sociologist Professor Helmut Schoeck, author of *Envy: A Theory of Social Behavior*, believes that child psychology, drawing on its studies of sibling jealousy, may help to explain why envy arises over small differences rather than big ones. We are more likely to feel really jealous of a neighbor who has a better car than ours than of the millionaire with a collection of Rolls-Royces, yachts and palatial homes. In so far as the disposition to envy is acquired mainly through suffering sibling rivalry, what is involved is almost a conditioned reflex towards the perception of small inequalities. Within a family group the coveted possession is generally similar to one already possessed (often it is, indeed, exactly the same and it is only in the resentful child's imagination that it appears bigger, better, newer or more expensive). Unconsciously the jealous individual almost *expects* that his emotion will be aroused by minimal differences between himself and another, just as it was during his childhood and adolescence.

Latent Envy

Dr. Benjamin Spock, in his book *Dr. Spock Talks with Mothers*, has this to say about the force of jealousy: "Of all the factors that make for ordinary quarreling between children, I think that jealousy is by far the most potent. The strongest attachment in childhood is of course the one between the child and his parents. To some degree he wants the parents' love for himself alone, and fears that the affection which goes out to brothers and sisters will be subtracted from his share. This makes him suspicious and resentful of them. We have to realize that this possessive, jealous element in love is not simply an unfortunate flaw in the character of man. It is part of the essence of our humanness. It's part of what makes us tick together as husband and wife, as families, and as other groups. Otherwise our relationships would be as casual as the relationships of insects."

This point is an interesting one. Professor Schoeck states that without envy there could be no social group of any size. The mutual and spontaneous supervision exercised by human beings over each other—in other words, social control—owes its effectiveness to the envy latent in all of us. If we were quite incapable of envy and, more important, if we were also convinced that our behavior would not be envied by anyone, that mutual exploration of the threshold of social tolerance—a constant social process upon which the predictability of social life depends—would never occur.

Sigmund Freud came to the conclusion that jealousy is an entirely normal phenomenon, a universal stage in the early development of personality. An older child may feel an intense jealousy towards a new baby. This does not always appear immediately; sometimes it comes when the baby begins to sit up and become more recognizably a "personality" to the older brother or sister. But certainly, the advent of a new member of the family is an alarming event. The near-monopoly position of the up-to-now "youngest one" (especially in the case of the firstborn) is broken. Often the baby demands so much time and care that the elder child really is deprived of even his fair share of attention. His fears are confirmed.

Cold Shoulder

In the excitement and bustle of bringing a new baby home, the other child is likely to feel left out and resentful. It may help if he is taken out for the day and comes home when all is calm and his mother has time to welcome him, preferably not with the baby in her arms. If certain changes have to be made around the house—if, for instance, he has to move into another room—it is important for him not to feel that he is being pushed out. It may be an idea to make whatever changes are necessary a few months before the baby is due. The youngster must be told that the baby is going to arrive, and the way the news is broken

Only when she's sure her mother has enough love to go around will she accept the demanding intruder.

PAF International

to him will help determine his attitude.

The first few weeks after the baby's arrival are important because the older child can easily form the impression that the household now revolves around the baby. His mother is forever busy with diapers and bottles and may seem to have no time for him. Visitors who used to make a fuss of him now immediately go to look at the baby instead. It does not have to be like this. Visitors can be tactfully discouraged from showing too much (or sole) interest in the baby. In any event babies sleep most of the time in the first few months and do not require constant attention, and they can often be fed and cared for while the older child is engrossed in a game and does not want attention.

If he is very young the child may make no secret of his rage and jealousy. He may show his hostility by making the infant cry or by saying uncomplimentary things about it. He may express resentment by being disobedient, rough, or babyish with his mother. In some instances, he may regress to an earlier phase, refusing food or wetting and soiling himself in an attempt to regain his parents' attention. Or he may be aggressive to the baby and seek an opportunity to harm him. If the parents fail to make allowances for this and are shocked by their elder child's bad behavior, or punish him for it, he may repress his jealousy. Older children are even more likely to feel guilty about their jealousy and hostility, repressing their feelings to such an extent that their parents

Once a pattern of rivalry is set up, the smallest slight ends in a row.

remain totally unaware of the conflict.

The best way to deal with jealousy is to accept it for what it is—a need for affection and reassurance, resulting from a sudden feeling of insecurity —and to give the child these things, within reasonable limits. At the same time he can be encouraged to be "grown-up." If he is reassured of his parents' affection, he will soon revert to his normal behavior. Some children adopt a parental attitude to the baby, wanting to help look after him. This may still be, in part, a way of dealing with jealous feelings by denying them. In taking a parental role, the child is saying that the baby's arrival does not threaten him. He will express the warmest affection to the baby and seem anxious to help nurse him. But if allowed to do so unsupervised, he may allow some accident to occur.

By learning to restrain—not merely repress—his jealous inclinations, a child takes a vital step towards maturity. This is why the feelings he has should not be suppressed by authoritarian, punitive methods, but be allowed to surface and work themselves out. Preoccupation with some unexpressed conflict may be evident from the way he talks about the baby much more than would be expected. The parent can try to give the child opportunities to talk about his feelings: it helps if the child can admit to himself that he feels jealous.

On the other hand, jealous acts have

to be kept in check in the general interest of the safety of the helpless baby and the peaceful atmosphere of the home. There has to be, in other words, a balance. There are dangers in either extreme—unbridled expression of jealousy and complete denial or inhibition of the emotion. Unless the child's feelings of insecurity and anger are brought into the open and coped with successfully, they can persist throughout childhood and affect his ability to deal with other jealousy-provoking situations he will meet later.

In dealing with open jealousy the mother has to do two things: make it quite clear that the child will not be allowed to hurt the baby, and at the same time reassure him that he is loved as much as ever and his jealous feelings are unfounded. In reassuring the child that he is loved the mother should not in any way apologize for the baby's presence—the child must realize that the baby has a right to be in the house. If parents react strongly to demonstrations of jealousy, this may increase the child's fear of rejection and may also cause him to conceal his jealousy in the future, which is not at all the same thing as controlling it. Such concealment merely increases a child's bitterness and makes it less likely that he will be able to control himself when he is finally left alone with the baby and can express his hostility.

Jealousy can lead to emotional disturbance in some circumstances. For an eleven-year-old girl named Pearl, a highly strung and emotional child, it resulted in nightmares and a refusal to go to school, where she was usually in trouble. When he was five, her little brother, of whom she had apparently been extraordinarily jealous, had fallen into a canal and been drowned. Pearl was not at home at the time but had taken his death very badly, and her parents dated her behavior difficulties from that time.

Pearl developed the habit of telling people—at every opportunity—about her brother's death, but the story she told was quite inaccurate. She would describe coming home from school, seeing her brother at the edge of the canal, and calling out to him—in this way she assumed actual responsibility for the accident because of the harmful wishes she secretly harbored against him. Her refusal to go to school and her flagrant misbehavior there were apparently punishment-seeking devices.

Jealous rivalry between older children has its roots in insecurity. Children are naturally competitive and they vie for parental favor. If they believe they are receiving less than other children, they feel threatened and may fight desperately for the affection they think they are missing. It is not whether a child has cause to be jealous that matters, but whether he *believes* he has. Children place great importance on matters of which adults are mostly quite unaware—who is going out with dad, who had the biggest helping.

A young child who feels that he is taking second place to another member of the family will usually make some attempt to win the attention which he believes is given to his rival. Jealous children often become excessively naughty to gain attention. Others become excessively good. However, a child may express his disturbance in a more indirect way, such as refusing to go to school, or he may become quiet and withdrawn.

Having learned that open jealousy of other members of the family is frowned on, he may suppress it but give vent to his feelings by expressing resentment of other children at school. Jealousy is almost self-fulfilling: it is such an ugly attribute that an openly jealous child is not particularly lovable. Rejecting a child by punishing him for being jealous is the most self-defeating approach. His fears must be allayed, not reinforced.

Jealousy is not restricted to children; competition for the children's love is one source of jealousy between husband and wife. Immature parents may vie with one another to win the love and preference of their offspring. This is likely to cause emotional conflict in the child, which becomes particularly oppressive and tragic when there is a separation or divorce.

Forgotten Fathers
A parent may feel envious of his or her child. The birth of the first child may sometimes arouse jealousy in the father, who feels he is being excluded from his wife's attention. An aging mother may feel a pang of jealousy when her husband spoils their teenage daughter, especially when she gets her way by being flirtatious.

It is obvious that the situations which provoke jealousy in adults are numerous. An older woman working with young girls may become jealous of the attention they receive from male colleagues. In heightened emotional settings like a hospital ward, one patient may excite jealous reactions if he seems to be getting more than his fair share of attention. Parents may resent those who take over the care of their children. Women who are childless are often jealous of their fertile friends. The later months of pregnancy are often associated with fits of jealousy.

Insatiable Appetite
The most fertile ground for jealousy to grow and prosper in is marriage. Jealousy between husband and wife can reach a state of such bitterness that the marriage can be undermined and the family fragmented. First, and most obvious, is sexual jealousy. Whether men and women—or whether women but not men—are by nature monogamous and endowed with a capacity for life-long fidelity is something which has long been argued, and the debate will no doubt continue. What is certain, however, is that a very large number of married men and women are unfaithful at some time or another, and this can cause a feeling of such intolerable jealousy in the other that forgiveness is very difficult, especially if one partner is more attractive than the other.

The major difficulty in coping with a jealous mate is that jealousy, unlike any of the other emotions which affect relationships, has an enormous, insatiable appetite. It can feed on *anything.* A husband's glance at a pretty girl in the street is fuel for his wife's jealousy. But his studied effort *not* to glance at a pretty girl can be taken in the same way.

If there are no real events on which it can feed, jealousy will find fuel in the imagination. Jealous people are prone to "come across" letters, photos, significant bills and receipts in which they can find a hidden meaning. In truth, they look for them. Similarly, they are extraordinarily receptive to "suspicious" looks.

Given that jealousy is part of normal life, both inside and outside the family, when is it abnormal? One means of evaluating it is to determine if there is a just cause and to ask, even if the provocation is real, whether the response is out of proportion to the cause. Is the person amenable to argument, or is every available piece of evidence, however tenuous, brought in to support the jealous accusations?

A husband may see in every word or glance which his wife directs towards another man a secret and seductive invitation. Because of his violent anger and jealousy, his wife, not unnaturally, may reject him sexually. If she does, he may think she has a lover and in his rage accuse her of infidelity. He may make wild accusations that she has men in the house while he is out, that she has to rush to the bathroom as soon as he comes in to rearrange her clothes. Any new clothes which she has are thought to be presents from lovers. Money which she earns or borrows is thought to be obtained immorally. In extreme cases, the husband may beat his wife to extract a confession from her or to punish her for the supposed crimes. When jealousy is irrational, when it has no foundation in reality, an obsessively jealous mate will, somehow and somewhere, find a reason in fantasy if not in fact.

Crime of Passion
When the causes of jealousy are founded on fact, and a person does behave in such a way that his partner feels threatened and humiliated as a direct result, the appropriate course of action is relatively simple. The partner who, without regard for the feeling of his mate, makes sexual conquests outside the relationship, or who is a compulsive flirt, is behaving in an irresponsible way. In a healthy relationship this should not happen. A mature person does not intentionally hurt someone he loves for selfish reasons. Frank and open discussion of the problem should reveal the cause of the unhappiness, and appropriate steps can be taken—if only one is creative enough to try.

Because jealousy may be experienced in countless circumstances and at different levels of intensity, there are a variety of ways in which it may be expressed, apart from voicing it. Sulking or withdrawing are both methods of showing how severe the reaction has been. In extreme cases, it may result in striking the rival, or in earlier times offering to fight a duel. The anger and tension which jealousy releases may be so great that the unfortunate recipient is killed. In fact, French law recognizes a lowered degree of responsibility in "crimes of passion." The rage, however, may damage only the one who is jealous.

Jealousy can have a constructive face, if we are willing to learn from it. It can stimulate people into new attitudes and fresh endeavors. It may teach us not to take our partners and children for granted. It may help us, when we see others achieving successes which we thought impossible, to recognize that there are potentialities of action which we, too, might reach. But it will do this only if the jealousy is restrained and kept within limits, so that it does not corrupt and destroy the best qualities of our humanity.

Son and lover

D. H. Lawrence's tragedy was that his disregard for conventional morality interested the public more than his writing. Even today it is his Oedipus complex which attracts attention.

D. H. Lawrence shocked his contemporaries and is still shocking those who today continue to misunderstand his attitudes to sex. He has been called bestial, depraved, decadent, a genius and a messiah. The quality of his writing has been praised and the sensuality of its content condemned. His books have been regarded by some as revelations; they have also been publicly banned.

Today he stands as one of the acknowledged great figures of English literature and yet, almost half a century after his death, critics and public alike still quibble about the morality of his message.

Finger on the Pulse

To many people, Lawrence is known only as the author of *Lady Chatterley's Lover*, and the public exposure of bigotry and false argument that surrounded the famous trial of the book at the beginning of the 1960s in Britain first brought Lawrence's name to their notice. More recently he has become known as the author of the book of the film *Women in Love*. Once again, the public and the critics have seized on the chance to air their inhibitions and set them for comparison against the values of the working-class son of a miner, who so accurately put his finger on the pulse and the moral disorder of his generation and in consequence brought down on himself their righteous indignation.

Lawrence was primarily concerned with the relationships between men and women. "I'll do my life work," he wrote in a letter to a friend, Sally Hopkin, in 1912, "sticking up for the love between man and woman." A year later, when his novel *Sons and Lovers* was published and when he was beginning to write *Women in Love*, he wrote in another letter, "I can only write what I feel pretty strongly about: and that at present is the relation between men and women. After all," he continued, perhaps a little melodramatically, "it is *the* problem today, the establishment of a new relation,

Far from the soot and grime of Nottingham, Lawrence eventually found peace of mind in New Mexico.

or the readjustment of the old one, between men and women."

Because of the depth of Lawrence's sensitivity and perception of the malaise that beset his generation—and has since followed us through

several generations—it was not easy at the time (and still may not be) to understand exactly what he was trying to say, what he was condemning, and what he was trying to establish in its place. It is, unfortunately, only *too* easy to interpret what he has to say in oversimplified terms; these oversimplifications have given rise to the misunderstandings of his attitudes.

For instance—and the example is central to Lawrence's thinking and the opposition to him—it was assumed by many of his contemporaries that Lawrence rejected the intellect in favor of the senses: a meeting of minds was nothing, they interpreted him as saying; the meeting of bodies was what mattered, pure and simple. It was difficult to find much objectionable, physical contact in *The Rainbow*, one of his earliest books, but nonetheless it was suppressed.

Drags It Down

The eminent author John Galsworthy read *The Rainbow* and found it "aesthetically detestable. As to the sexual aspect," he wrote, "the writer forgets—as no great artist does—that by dwelling on the sexual side of life so lovingly he falsifies all the values of his work—for this reason if for no other: the sexual instinct is so strong in all of us that any emphasis upon it drags the whole being of the reader away from seeing life steadily, truly and whole; drags it away from the rest of the book, stultifies the writer's own efforts at the presentation of human life and character."

When *Sons and Lovers* appeared, Galsworthy acknowledged that there was genius in the book but once again resented the intrusion, as he put it, of the sexual passages. "The body's never worthwhile," he wrote in a letter, "and the sooner Lawrence recognizes that, the better. . . ." Lawrence disagreed entirely. It was just this dry intellectualism that repelled him, the idea that the real values of life excluded the body.

To Lawrence, morality was a reverence for a naturalistic life; sex seemed essential to fulfill life and human relationships. Not only was a relationship without sex barren, but a relationship that did not openly acknowledge the value of sex as a component part of any relationship was equally barren.

Lawrence's contemporaries missed the point. What they heard was "Take sex for a bit of pleasure"—a disruptive, morally undermining attitude that was far from Lawrence's preaching. He himself condemned "sex for sheer pleasure." Those of his characters who indulged in sex as their only means of communication, or solely

The house Lawrence was born in. Prior to his birth his mother kept a shop in the front room.

for satisfaction, he does not approve.

Gudrun and Gerald, who use sex as the last resort to keep them together in *Women in Love*, do not achieve happiness. In *Lady Chatterley's Lover*, the relationship between Lady Chatterley and the artist Michaelis is also doomed, because both are seeking little more than temporary satisfaction.

Lawrence spurned love for the sake of having someone to love just as much as he rejected sex for the sake of sex; love and sex as the be-all and

end-all of existence was not, as many seemed to believe, the morality he was preaching. Love and sex were not, to him, merely the means to the end of security; they were not the "means" to anything, except insofar as Lawrence set his characters, as sexual beings, against the dehumanization and artificiality of the industrial world, which he hated and feared as the source of all moral evil.

Love and sex were part of life, without which life was meaningless. To

Lawrence, sex itself, and the relationship between two people, was a process of reunification with nature, a harmonizing process that was spontaneous and liberating for the individual and the couple.

It was no good. Explanations of this kind sounded false to the critics and the public; they picked on the purple passages. They did not wish to be called hollow, dead, unloving, without tenderness, themselves immoral. To them, the philosophy that Lawrence expounded was the voice of the libertine. Everything he said sounded like a good excuse to indulge in sensuality. When *Women in Love* appeared, the critics had a field day. "A frenzy of sexual awareness," wrote J. M. Murry, "bestial, a thing that our forefathers had rejected when they began to rise from the slime."

One of the most infamous reviews of the book was by W. Charles Pilley, in *John Bull* magazine, and carried the banner headline "A Book the Police Should Ban: loathsome study of sex and depravity—misleading youth to unspeakable disaster." The author of the article did not claim to be a literary critic but, he wrote, "I know dirt when I smell it and here it is in heaps—festering, putrid heaps which smell to high heaven."

Today, a review like this would ensure any book a place in the best-seller lists. "In real life we should not be troubled with Mr. Lawrence's characters—they would be safely under lock and key. For instance, there is the idiot who undresses and wallows in wet grass, delighting to have his back scratched with thistles and his skin lacerated with the sharp points of fir cones. Doctors have a name for this sort of thing which at the moment I do not recall. Then there is the female degenerate who half kills her lover in a fit of frenzy and, as she strikes the blow, feels a 'delirium of pleasure' because, as she tells herself, she is going at last to her consummation of voluptuous ecstasy.

Sheer Filth

"We know well enough where this sort of thing leads to in real life. Criminal lawyers know all about it. It is precisely the mania that keeps the jails full and the hangman busy. . . . The book reeks of Bedlam horrors, . . . an epic of vice. . . . The chapter headed 'Gladiatorial' (in which the two men wrestle nude together) is sheer filth from beginning to end. . . . This is the sort of book which, in the hands of a boy in his teens, might pave the way to unspeakable moral disaster."

Contrast this with Lawrence's own comment in his foreword to the book: "Lewdness is hateful because it impairs our integrity and our proud being." Obviously, this misunderstanding between himself and his detractors was an unbridgeable gulf. That gulf has never been narrowed.

The points of difference between Lawrence and his contemporaries arose from more than his novels. It did not help that the subject he chose to write about was still largely regarded as taboo by so-called civilized society. It helped even less that the man who so dogmatically wrote about the subject came from the working classes and was therefore considered by many of the literate public to be naturally incapable of appreciating the finer and higher points of love: it was no wonder that "sensitive"

Lydia Lawrence, the writer's mother, exerted a powerful influence on her son until her death in 1910.

readers saw in his elevation of sensual experience nothing more than an indulgence in the fundamental sexual animalism that could only be expected of the lower classes.

Lawrence wrote at a time when class distinctions in Britain were still very strong. He was regarded with suspicion by those who could not understand how he could possibly *be* a genius with his background—and with incomprehension by those who recognized the work of a genius but viewed his message with apprehension.

Lawrence did not try to make his way easier. Just as he believed—as was apparent in the treatment his books received—that England had rejected him, so he rejected England. He spent ten years of his most fruitful writing period outside the country.

Born in Eastwood, Nottinghamshire, in September, 1885, Lawrence was the fourth of five children. Eastwood was a small mining village and Lawrence's father worked in the local colliery. The class conflicts that run so fiercely through Lawrence's novels began early in his life, for though his father was rooted in the working classes, his mother had once been a schoolteacher and came from a relatively prosperous family. His parents' marriage was not very happy; they quarreled continually about the manner and the extent of their children's education, Lawrence's mother always wanting more for them than their father thought proper or necessary.

It was inevitable that the intelligent and inquiring Lawrence should become devoted to his mother and reject his father and a great deal of what he stood for. His close relationship with his mother was reflected in *Sons and Lovers,* a largely autobiographical novel, in which the son is torn between love for his mother and a girl.

The girl, in real life, was Jessie Chambers, the daughter of a neighboring family and a powerful influence on Lawrence as he grew up. Jessie encouraged his writing and received in turn repeated assurance that everything he wrote was done for her. After the novel was published, Jessie was so upset at the treatment she received in the story that she never communicated with Lawrence again.

Sudden Elopement

He left school in 1901, worked briefly for a surgical appliance manufacturer, fell ill with pneumonia, and then became a pupil-teacher in Eastwood and subsequently at Ilkeston. After coming out top in the whole of England and Wales in a King's Scholarship examination in 1904, he went to Nottingham University College, which he left in 1908. His mother died two years later, an event that shattered what remaining links he had with his background village and brought, in consequence, the resentment of his working class contemporaries, who believed that he was betraying them and misusing his education.

But an even more dramatic and far-reaching event occurred in 1912, when Lawrence met the German wife of his former professor of French at Nottingham University, Ernest Weekley, and fell in love. Her name was Frieda, the daughter of Friedrich von Richthofen and cousin to the "Red Baron." Within only a few weeks of their meeting, Frieda and Lawrence went off to Germany. They married two years later, when her divorce was made final.

It was just the sort of thing that Lawrence's detractors might have expected from him. For a young man to go off with an older, married woman was a far more shocking event than we can possibly imagine today. Many critics implied that it was just another

K. Werner

Frieda von Richthofen became the new female influence in Lawrence's life after their first meeting in 1912.

gesture of defiance. This was unfair. Through happy and difficult times, the couple stayed together until Lawrence's death in 1930.

Their marriage marked another rupture with Lawrence's past, emphasized by the publication of *Sons and Lovers* in 1913, and by Lawrence's attitude to World War I, which broke out the following year. He utterly condemned the war, though he was lucky enough not to have to argue his case in court as his physical condition anyway made him unfit for service. In *The Rainbow*, he referred to "wooden soldiers," and it may have been this reference as much as the sexual scenes that brought about the banning of the book.

The couple spent some time traveling in Italy and Germany and finally left England completely in 1919. The rest of Lawrence's life was spent in a search for fresh roots, which he came nearest to finding in New Mexico, after visiting first Ceylon and then Australia. After three years in New Mexico, he returned to Europe. He died in March, 1930, in Venice.

The public outrage over Lawrence continued long after his death. Half the trouble was that he did not care whom he offended. He wished to stir people out of their complacency, their soulless relationships; he scorned those who could not take his writing.

In 1917 he wrote to the American poet Amy Lowell, "Nobody will publish *Women in Love*—my best bit of work. The publishers say that it is too strong for an English public. Poor darling English public, when will it go in for a little spiritual athletics?"

Trial of Taboos

And when his paintings were exhibited in London in 1929, the year after the publication of *Lady Chatterley's Lover,* and received an outcry of indignation because the nudes possessed sexual organs and pubic hair, Lawrence wrote a collection of poems called "Gross, Coarse, Hideous (Police Description of My Pictures)", one of which had a verse:

Lately *I* saw a sight most quaint:
London's lily-like policemen faint
in virgin outrage as they viewed
the nudity of a Lawrence nude.

But it was *Lady Chatterley's Lover* that aroused the greatest debate of all Lawrence's work. When the un-expurgated edition of the book was put on trial in the early 1960s, it was not just Lawrence that was in the

***Flight Back into Paradise:* like his writing, Lawrence's painting was bold and explicit.**

dock: it was the moral attitudes of the whole of society, more than thirty years after Lawrence himself had attempted to readjust them. The central theme of the story—the relationship between Lady Chatterley and the gamekeeper was known to everyone.

The arguments in favor and against the book ranged between literary merit and moral degeneration—as they always had. No one cared much about the values of life expressed in the book; the case was a test of public morals, a trial of permissiveness, a trial of taboos. After the trial, when the bookshops were stacked with copies, there were record-breaking lines in the streets.

When Lawrence became legal tender, he was not understood any better. The license to sex that the trial ostensibly granted was not a moral value of any worth, certainly not one Lawrence himself expounded. It was bereft of tenderness; it did not occur as a natural development in a relationship; it was as artificial in its way as the values he had deplored.

A dirty business

"They've paved paradise and put up a parking lot." Cars take precedence over trees in the consumer society, and in the pursuit of happiness we have polluted our air and water and turned our cities into garbage dumps. But it's not only ugly . . . it's lethal.

Every time you go out in your car you are contributing to a sequence of atmospheric changes which may cause the polar ice caps to melt and eventually to flood the very road you are driving along. Each time you throw away a carton, a bottle, or a can, you may be signing the death warrant of thousands of fish or water plants in a neighboring river or estuary. With each mouthful of a breakfast cereal, you may be condoning the killing of birds, animals, insects, plants, organisms and microorganisms, which you depend on for next year's breakfasts.

The connecting link between these commonplace occurrences and their astonishing consequences is pollution. At the point of consumption you finish off a process of pollution which began with the gathering of the raw material and continued in the stages of production, packaging and distribution, through which any article you buy must go. Then in discarding its wrapping, its residue, and ultimately the product itself, you start off another.

The rapid rise in the world's population has been accompanied by an even greater increase in the demands which man has made on the earth's natural resources. Using technology, both in industry and agriculture, he has aimed to secure for himself not only an adequate supply of the necessities of life—food and shelter—but also the additional advantages of power, mobility, leisure, security, longevity and all the luxuries which make for a high standard of living.

Tampering with Nature

To achieve these goals he has devised ingenious ways of maximizing the earth's resources and of converting them to his needs by industrial processes. But in so doing he has compelled nature to do two things which it is not necessarily obliged to do: he forces the environment to produce more than its usual quota of resources, and to take back unprecedented quantities of waste products when man and his technology have done with them. It is when nature fails to come up to these expectations that pollution occurs.

The word "pollution" means "contamination"; the word "contamination" means "defiling by touching and mixing." By touching the environment with advanced technology, tampering with nature's time-tested self-renewing systems, and introducing "foreign bodies" in the form of synthetic compounds and chemicals, we have injected a virus to which our planet is not immune, and from which it might never recover.

Death Warrant

The signs of this contamination are everywhere. The casualties are fish destroyed and washed up on ocean shores into which industrial plants have disgorged their poisons; sea birds with their wings gummed up by jettisoned oil from a leaking supertanker; feathered or furred creatures whose life-support systems in woodlands and hedgerows have been obliterated by man's ambitious construction programs; benevolent insects which found themselves in the firing line of pesticide sprays intended for their malicious neighbors; trees, flowers, and plants choked into oblivion by exhaust fumes from roadways and air corridors. Already the death toll is huge, and these casualties constitute the thin end of a very thick wedge.

Supposedly, these misfortunes are all for the benefit of man. But man himself has not escaped the consequences. People have died from mercury poisoning after eating contaminated tuna fish, others from eating the meat of pigs accidentally fed seeds coated with poison intended for crop-destroying insects. Excess lead content in water supplies has permanently blighted some lives—causing nausea, nervousness, and insanity—while others have been foreshortened by the constant intake of polluted air which leads to heart disease, bronchitis, emphysema, and cancer. In terms of output, the case for advanced technology in industry and agriculture has been proved; but we have to be sure that the sacrifice of animal, plant, and human life has not been in vain and that the overall benefit is lasting.

That case is still before the open court.

First and foremost, people require food. The widespread starvation and undernourishment in the contemporary world shows that agricultural technology has fallen far short of its goals. To achieve them it needs heavy machinery to take on the back-breaking labor of plowing, sowing, and harvesting; fertilizers to add nutrients to the soil; and pesticides to ensure that the farmer gets to his crop before nature's predators. But each of these introduces elements into the farming process which have no established links with the traditional and natural production system. The weight of heavy machinery which discharges oil fumes close to the ground may be slowly destroying the texture of the earth beyond self-repair. Impregnation of chemical fertilizers, intended to boost the growth and to compensate the land for previous overexertion, may be gradually undermining the natural goodness of the soil and irrevocably reducing a crop's ability to reproduce in its own good time. Furthermore they seep into waterways to infect aquatic life there.

Pests That Protect

Pesticides—DDT and other chlorinated hydrocarbons like Dieldrin and Endrin—are sprayed over vast acreages of arable land and shoot much wider than their mark. Along with pests—flies and insects carrying disease to livestock or destroying crops—perish creatures and plants which far from doing the crops harm actually make a positive contribution to their growth. The same goes for herbicides, which if indiscriminately used destroy vegetation that is either beneficial in itself or protects the soil from erosion.

Nature is an integrated whole. Its regenerative cycle depends on a chain of events in which every living organism participates, each reproducing itself, but also in life and death contributing to the survival of the next in line in the natural hierarchy. An insect which lives on plants is devoured by another creature which in turn becomes the victim of a larger predator, whose waste products and ultimately his own body are consumed by microbes which feed the soil where the plants grow, and so on. The survival of life depends on the natural cycle being followed through, so that every creature gives back to nature what he has taken out. But man has interfered with this system.

By destroying whole populations of pests he removes from the natural cycle something which was there before; and in doing so with chemical and synthetic substances he introduces something which was *not* there before. That new element is a killer, a contamination which far from dying with its victim is passed from one organism to another, and will subsequently find its way into the soil, into the waterways, or into the air.

Bring Back the Cats
All pollution, to a greater or lesser degree, has its impact not just on a part of the natural cycle but on the whole system. By wiping out one species you also starve into extinction another which preyed upon it. You also have on your hands a population explosion of some creature whose numbers the pest you have destroyed kept down, which may be even more damaging to crops. A graphic illustration of such a sequence of events was experienced in a Bolivian town, where DDT was sprayed to control malaria-carrying mosquitoes. It also killed most of the local cats, whose absence was exploited by rats who invaded the town carrying black typhus, which killed several hundred people before the cats were restored.

In this case it was easy to relate cause and effect and to see how the balance of nature had been disturbed. Not so easy to see, though, are similar disruptions occurring at the level of microorganisms, but there is no doubt that any pollution or contamination introduced higher up the scale will filter down to them. And it is there that the most damage might be done.

Once you have unleashed a poison into the environment it is bound to reappear sooner or later. If sooner, the results are obvious—like the ten to fifteen million fish killed by the pesticide Endrin leaking into the Mississippi River in the 1960s. If later, it is not always clear where the damage has been done or what caused it. For instance, species which are most exposed to some chemical may build up an immunity to it, so that it does not kill until it has passed through the food chain to a less resistant creature.

If it does not destroy it, the substance may affect it in some other way. For instance, it is known that some birds, as a result of chemical intake, lay eggs with shells so thin that they crack when laid. It may be years before the full impact of that reduced bird population is felt.

Chemicals are sometimes long-lived. Malathion—an insecticide used on fruits—has survived eight months in cold storage without losing any of its potency. Some chemicals are given not only to longevity, but also to wanderlust—and turn up in the most unlikely places miles away from their starting point. For example, DDT has been found in penguins living thousands of miles from where it was used.

So, in order to appreciate the full effect of pollution, we have to look far beyond immediate horizons. This is why it is causing such alarm among environmentalists and public-spirited citizens. It can be assumed that the damage it is doing on the surface is not as severe as the contamination which, unseen and unbeknown to us, is infecting the very foundations of our life-support system. Since this deeper penetration into the environment takes time, we can be sure that some of the most serious repercussions of pollution which occurred long ago have yet to be felt.

Nobody denies that insecticides and fertilizers have a perfectly legitimate function, but what we must be on our guard against is indiscriminate and careless overuse. We must also heed the warning—first sounded by Rachel Carson in her pioneering book *Silent Spring*, which was mainly concerned with deleterious side effects of pesticides—that more research and more knowledge is needed before we can be sure that scientific exploitation of resources is of long-term value.

Pollution Power
Far harder to justify, though, is injecting the waste products of industry into the environment. Next to food, the most pressing demand of technological man is for power and energy to drive his factories and machines. Power plants are the greatest contributors to the pollution of the atmosphere: most of the world's energy supplies come from the combustion of coal and other fossil fuels which give off sulphur dioxide, oxides of nitrogen, and soot and ash into the air.

These combine to cause disease, get people and property dirty, absorb sunlight, and reduce visibility on the ground. Add the carbon monoxide from oil-burning plants and from that arch polluter, the motor car, to the accumulation of toxic gases in the atmosphere, and the consequences are infinitely more far-reaching. Every ton of wood coal burned releases *several* tons of carbon dioxide into the atmosphere. Its effect is to allow sunlight to reach the earth but to limit the reradiation of the generated heat back into space. The temperature of the earth therefore rises, and it might in the not too distant future be enough to melt the polar ice cap, raising the sea level by 400 feet.

Radioactive Rain
As coal and oil resources are being depleted, scientists are having to look for alternative means of power. Some, like tidal barrages, thermal power, or solar energy will be low on pollution, but nuclear power could turn out to be the most dangerous source of energy yet devised. Fallout from nuclear tests contaminates every part of the earth's surface and all living things upon it. Strontium 90 is just one of the radioactive isotopes rained down from the stratosphere to the earth, penetrating the soil and passing through plants to animals, and eventually to man, causing genetic damage or cancer.

Arctic Eskimos, found to have high levels of fallout radioactivity in their bodies, show how this dangerous substance passes through the food chain. Lichens, which grow on rocks, draw their nutrients from the air absorbing the fallout. They in turn are eaten in large quantities by caribous, which provide the Eskimos' diet.

The generation of nuclear power for industrial purposes presents two hazards. The first is from thermal pollution, the discharge of hot water from cooling processes into oceans and rivers: fish and other aquatic life are particularly susceptible to sudden changes in temperature. The other danger is that some radioactive elements in gases and effluent might seep into the atmosphere. The amount may be small, and every effort is made to contain all the radioactivity given off in nuclear power generation. Some elements are short-lived, but others have a lifetime of thousands of years, and there is always the danger of some major breakdown when the safeguards may prove inadequate.

Top right: When herbivorous animals find their food source depleted, the fine balance of nature is disturbed and a chain reaction leads to soil erosion. Right: Public Enemy No. 1— wanted for air pollution and noise. Far right: A breathtaking view.

Friends of the Earth

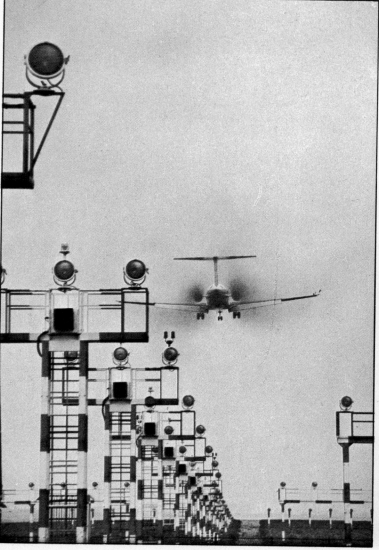

Friends of the Earth

The very same land and waterways which are required to dispose of increasing amounts of industrial wastes also serve the cities which house the industrial labor force. Large concentrations of people demand more power, more food, and more goods, and the greater quantities of effluent, sewage, and detergents are often more than the natural disposal systems can cope with. Dissolved oxygen is the main agent of natural decomposition in water, and bacteria which break down waste matter depend on it; so does all aquatic life. But it is not in unlimited supply, and nothing can survive once all the oxygen has been used up, except certain bacteria which effuse repulsive gases.

But the job of decomposition is still not done. Having destroyed all life which might eventually have broken it down, waste matter just accumulates, turning the waterways into lifeless, stagnant sewers. Also choking them up are the inorganic materials which cannot be decomposed.

The growth of industry and the cities has led to a geographical separation of the consumer from his supplies of food and materials. This makes further demands which technology must fulfill: transportation, distribution, and packaging. The motor car—apart from being a hazard to life and limb —is a great polluter of the air, particularly in the cities where the atmosphere is already overloaded with toxic emissions from industrial and domestic chimney stacks. Vast stretches of good productive agricultural land must be torn up to build roads and to clear sites for their ancillary services, exposing the neighboring land and its wild life to the exhaust fumes of vehicles and the waste products of a mobile people.

Throwaway Needs

The packaging industry makes a very substantial contribution to the pollution of the environment. As a heavy industry, some is caused at the production stage when bottles, cartons, tin cans, and other containers are made. In 1970, the United States produced 60 million tons of packaging materials, but it is the fact that over 90 percent of that output will be discarded after a very short life which sets the packaging industry apart.

Estimates vary as to how much garbage we throw away, but most people agree it is excessive. In the United States, the total is more than one billion pounds of solid waste a day, or one ton per head of population in a year. A typical breakdown shows that this waste is composed of 7 million cars, 100 million tires, 30 million tons of paper, 4 million tons of plastics, 48 billion cans, 26 billion bottles, and hundreds of thousands of obsolete domestic appliances.

The obvious question is: Where does it all go? The answer is equally obvious: Into the environment. But few of these materials go "back to nature" in a form which is beneficial to the natural cycle. Some are burned, contaminating the air; some are buried, polluting the land; some are poured into overburdened waterways.

To breathe clean air, to drink pure water, to eat uncontaminated food, and to enjoy natural beauty have always been inalienable human rights. The rights to possess material goods, to move about at speed, to produce and consume, and to strive towards greater wealth and leisure are all perfectly legitimate, but only insofar as they do not conflict with our priorities. The right to pollute the environment in pursuit of these goals cannot be guaranteed—or justified.

One drop of oil from a leaking tanker is enough to gum up a sea bird's wings.

Friends of the Earth

John Watney

Mother knows best

The way our parents shape us is the crucial factor in determining how well we fit into society.

Adaptation is a concept which is central to Charles Darwin's theory of evolution. Over countless thousands of years, new species appeared and flourished because genetic mutations allowed some forms of life to *adapt* better than others.

Even in the psychological realm the slogan might be "Adapt or perish." Those whose adjustive mechanisms are defective (for example, the severely subnormal or the mentally ill) have to be taken care of in special institutions because they cannot survive in the outside world. There are many individuals who cannot make the necessary adjustments to life and opt out of it by committing suicide. And there are countless others who survive, but whose survival is so marginal that they are barely existing. Feeling as they do—alienated, un-

loved, unreal and aimless—they cannot be said to be living life to the full.

Each person discovers and evolves his own set of strategies to cope with life. But no two approaches are the same and there are great difficulties in defining effective adjustment. *How* an individual behaves depends upon both the situation he finds himself in and the adjustive strategies he brings to that situation, which consist of various attitudes, skills, abilities.

In a survey of 275 American families, nearly all the mothers reported a number of undesirable forms of behavior in their children. Problem behavior tends to be very annoying, but this does not necessarily mean that all behaviors which annoy and create problems are to be equated with maladjustment. Parents vary in what they can tolerate in the way of "bad"

behavior. The eminent child psychiatrist Leo Kanner observed that "the high annoyance threshold of many fond and fondly resourceful parents keeps away from clinics . . . a multitude of early breath-holders, nail-biters, nose-pickers and casual masturbators who, largely because of this kind of parental attitude, develop into reasonably happy and well-adjusted adults." It has been found that the reason behind referring a child to a guidance clinic is as closely related to the reactions of his *parents* (that is, whether they are anxious, easily upset and lacking in ability to cope with children) as to whether *he* actually has a problem.

Margaret Mead's work among the South Sea Islanders showed how different styles of upbringing create variations in patterns of adjustment.

The Arapesh of New Guinea are quiet, gentle, peace-loving people, among whom self-assertion is so rare as to be regarded as abnormal. For their periodic celebrations, they have to force some of their members, much against their will, into the role of organizers. Passivity and selflessness form an essential part of the nurture and education of each individual. From birth, the child observes these traits in those about him and, during the course of his development, integrates them into his own personality.

Code of Behavior

In complete contrast, another island group, the Mundugumor, fosters aggression from infancy. If a suckling baby does not take a firm grip on his mother's breast, she will pull the nipple away and the infant will go hungry. As a child grows up his early experience is reinforced by training in warlike pursuits. In other tribes, women were found to assume the dominant role and do the important work; men were submissive and responsible only for domestic tasks.

A stable home and the presence of both a mother and a father are generally thought to be necessary influences for healthy development of the child's personality. Notions of right and wrong, a code of behavior, a set of attitudes and values, the ability to see the other person's point of view —all these basic qualities which mold an individual into a socialized personality flow in the first instance from the family setting.

The psychologist Gordon Allport describes two aspects of the developing self-image: the way the individual sees his present abilities, status and roles; and what he would like to become, his aspirations for himself—in other words, his idealized self-image. Research studies consistently indicate that personal happiness and satisfaction in life depend on a reasonable agreement between the present and the idealized self-concept. Marked discrepancies arouse anxiety; they are a feature of neurotic personalities and occur commonly in the psychological crises of middle age.

An individual's self-esteem is also shaped by his ability to perceive how other people see him and to compare his image of himself with what he believes others expect of him. The individual's perception of the way he appears to a particular group of other people or one significant other person, has been termed his "subjective public identity." One person may have as many such identities as there are

PAF International

groups of significant people he believes perceive him in a distinctive way.

There is a marked variation in the degree of permanence and stability with which the self is organized. Some individuals have a very loosely organized pattern of different selves, with only a small core of common elements to all. Such a chameleonlike person is described as "poorly integrated." His self consists of the various roles he characteristically plays.

Parental love and affection during early life and their unfolding attitudes toward the child as he copes with his impulses and failures are of import-

Fathers are especially useful when you're too tired to go it alone.

ance in the more and more sophisticated evolution of his self-image. The expressed attitudes and behavior of everyone in the family provide him with information about his mastery, goodness and worth. Living up to parental expectations (or always failing to do so in the case of overcritical or hostile parents) becomes part of his self-concept.

Dr. P. M. Symonds, an American psychologist, published a comprehensive review of findings in the

2238

1930s, based on many years of experimental and observational research, concerning parent-child relationships. Two major dimensions—acceptance-rejection and dominance-submission—emerged from this work. Children of submissive parents appeared to be more aggressive, stubborn and disorderly, although more self-confident than the offspring of dominating parents. Dominating parents tended to produce children who were more sensitive, submissive, orderly and polite, better socialized but more dependent. Children who were accepted seemed to manifest characteristics which are generally thought desirable, while those who were rejected were reported to be more neurotic, rebellious and delinquent.

Ideal Mother

More recent studies of parent-child relations have concentrated on the same themes but are made more precise by the application of special psychological instruments; computer techniques have also been used to reduce the rich variety of childhood and parental behaviors to a few main dimensions. Two main underlying components of parental attitudes and behaviors still emerge from many of the studies: firstly, attitudes which are "warm" (or loving) at one extreme, and "rejecting" (or hostile) at the other; secondly, attitudes which are restrictive (controlling) at one extreme, and permissive (encouraging autonomy) at the other.

Dr. Earl Schaefer, a development psychologist, describes parental behavior in terms of the interactions of the two main attributes, thus a "democratic" mother is one who is both loving and permissive; an "antagonistic" mother combines hostility and restrictiveness; a "protective" mother is both loving and restrictive, and so on.

According to the researches of psychologist Dr. Diana Baumrind, a "permissive" mother is one who attempts to behave in a nonpunitive, accepting, and affirmative manner toward her child's impulses, desires, and actions. She consults with him about policy decisions and gives explanations for family rules, making few demands for household responsibility and orderly behavior. She presents herself to the child as someone to call upon for help and company as he wishes, not simply as an active agent responsible only for shaping or altering his ongoing or future behavior.

Practical skills like cooking are best taught informally at home.

havior. The "permissive" mother allows the child to regulate his own activities as much as possible, avoids the excessive exercise of control, and does not encourage him to obey absolute, externally defined standards. She attempts to use reason instead of overt power to accomplish her ends.

This empirical analysis is very different from the popular usage of the word "permissiveness," which tends to be reserved for the extreme end of the dimension with its connotations of lax discipline, unbridled license, and only too often indifference.

According to Dr. Baumrind the "restrictive" or "authoritarian" mother (as she emerges from detailed investigations) is one who attempts to shape, control, and assess the behavior and attitudes of her child according to a set standard of conduct, usually an absolute standard, motivated by theological considerations and formulated by a higher authority. She values obedience as a virtue and favors punitive, forceful measures to curb self-will at those points where the child's actions or beliefs conflict with her idea of proper conduct. She believes in indoctrinating the child with such values as respect for authority, respect for work, and respect for the preservation of traditional order. She does not encourage verbal give-and-take, believing that the child should accept her word for what is right.

Reviews of research into child-rearing techniques suggest that there is a happy medium and that the extremes of permissiveness and restrictiveness entail risks. A blend of permissiveness and a warm, encouraging, and accepting attitude fits the recommendations of child-rearing specialists who are concerned with fostering the sort of children who are socially outgoing, friendly, creative, and reasonably independent and self-assertive. Warm, loving, and consistent discipline, in which (when the child can understand them) reasons are given, is thought to produce a rational sort of obedience rather than a blind and emotionally dependent following of orders.

Recognition of Rights

The balance is perhaps best illustrated in the philosophy of what Baumrind calls the "authoritative parent." This kind of mother attempts to direct her child's activities in a rational manner determined by the issues involved in any particular disciplinary situation. She encourages verbal give-and-take and shares with the child the reasoning behind her policy. She values both the child's self-expression and his so-called "instrumental attributes" (respect for authority, work, and so on); she appreciates both independent self-will and disciplined conformity. Therefore, she exerts firm control at points where she and the child diverge in viewpoint, but does not hem in the child with restrictions. She recognizes her own special rights as an adult, but also the child's individual interests

and special ways personal to himself.

The "authoritative parent" affirms the child's present qualities, but also sets standards for future conduct. She uses reason as well as power to achieve her objectives. She does not base her decisions solely on the consensus of the group or the individual child's desires; but she also does not regard herself as infallible or divinely inspired. Baumrind found that authoritative parents are most likely to facilitate the development of competence and self-reliance in young children by enhancing responsible, purposive, and independent behavior.

Tinker, Tailor . . .

In the wake of thinkers like Pavlov, almost exclusive emphasis has been placed on environmental influences in the development of behavior. And parents, being the major feature of the child's early environment, received all the blame when things went wrong. But possessing certain combinations of temperamental qualities can make a child exceedingly "difficult" no matter how skilled the parents are.

John B. Watson, a psychologist at Johns Hopkins University during the first decades of the century, believed that planned habit training could mold the child in any desired direction. This is how he expressed it: "Give me a dozen healthy infants, well-formed, and my own specified world to bring them up in, and I'll guarantee to take any one at random and train him to become any type of specialist I might select—doctor, lawyer, artist, merchant-chief, and yes, even beggarman and thief, regardless of his talents, penchants, tendencies, abilities, vocations, and race of his ancestors." He discounted the influence of differences in children's individual capacities and their reactions to their environment. Environment *is* vital in determining individual differences, but it should not be forgotten that inborn attributes are also significant.

Bearing these inborn limitations and tendencies in mind, it still is undoubtedly possible for parents to instill certain qualities in their offspring. Most parents wish their children to grow up unselfish. British psychologist Derek Wright lists the main family influences that promote this crucial aspect of humane and compassionate behavior. "First, there must be a warm and affectionate relationship between parents and child. This provides the setting in which empathic responsiveness is most effectively learned and gives the first major incentive for altruistic action in the child's life. Secondly, the parents must themselves be sympathetic, both to the child and to others, and set a good example of altruistic action. The child can then learn through imitation a full repertoire of altruistic patterns of behavior. Thirdly, as the child grows older, his parents need to provide him with a rationale for altruistic tendencies to people outside his immediate circle of family and friends."

Outlet for Aggression

Parents also wish their children to grow up to be morally aware. Dr. M. L. Hoffman, a developmental theorist, believes that all disciplinary encounters have a great deal in common, regardless of the specific technique used. They all have three components, one or the other of which may predominate: power assertion; love withdrawal, and induction. Hoffman contends that the most reliable finding in parent-child research is the negative relationship between power assertion and moral behavior. Punitive techniques are self-defeating.

Parental disapproval and the child's subsequent anxiety about losing their love are the major contributing factors to the child's internalization of parental values. There is evidence that this love withdrawal may contribute to the inhibition of anger, for it produces anxiety which leads to the renunciation of hostile and possibly other impulses. However, although Hoffman recognizes the contribution of love withdrawal in making the child more susceptible to adult influence, he maintains that this does not necessarily affect moral development.

Induction is the type of discipline Hoffman finds most conducive to moral development. It involves pointing out the effects of the child's behavior, giving reasons and explanations. To be effective the disciplinary technique must enlist already existing emotional and motivational tendencies within the child. In other words, a basis of affection must fuel the child's need for approval and hence his readiness to attend to and heed what is being conveyed to him. All three of these disciplinary techniques communicate some negative evaluation by the parent and are thus likely to elicit the child's need for approval.

PAF International

Like riding a bicycle, bringing up children is a question of balance.

Love's labors lost

Rechanneling your sex drive is fine as long as there's a light at the end of the tunnel.

The standards of Western culture simply will not allow us to give vent to all our sexual urges whenever we please. Unfortunately, the laws of nature are not so easily contravened by the dictates of society, and there is trouble ahead if this tremendous instinctual energy does not somehow find an acceptable outlet.

Sexual sublimation is the unconscious process by which repressed energy of sexual impulses is diverted towards new aims and activities. Most of us have experienced it at some time in our lives—unless we have given full rein to every sexual desire from our childhood onwards.

An adolescent in our culture is unlikely to be able to satisfy his new-found sexual appetite through the usual channels available to adults, such as intercourse or other more sophisticated means of sexual gratification. He may not even masturbate, either because he does not know how or because the atmosphere he has been raised in is hostile or repressive towards this quite normal activity.

The Boy Scout movement, for example, while encouraging boys to acquire various skills and exhorting them to exemplify the ideals of Christian behavior, positively discouraged its members from either thinking about or expressing their sexuality. Boys were told to stifle their ''unnatural desires'' and to take cold showers instead—advice which many modern psychiatrists would view as positively harmful to the boy's psyche, since guilt and repression at this age may have a permanent effect on future attitudes to sex.

This is not to say that it would be desirable to encourage teenagers to indulge their sexual desires to the full, even though there is evidence to suggest that the age when they first have sexual intercourse is nonetheless getting steadily lower over the years. But to deny the existence of a strong sexual urge at and immediately after puberty is equally wrong.

Possibly the most obvious exponents of the art of sublimation exist in those religious orders where the members have chosen or been compelled to accept chastity as a way of life.

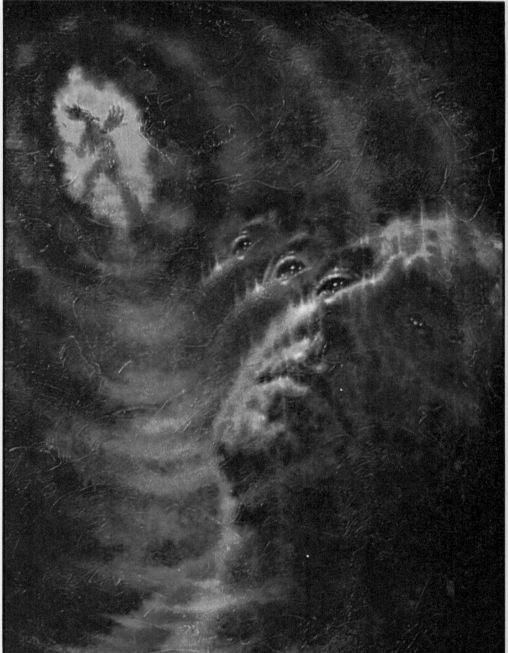

Bradford Boobis

An ordained Roman Catholic priest, for example, has to forego any sexual relationships with women, as does a nun with men. Whether or not homosexuality or autostimulation occurs among these celibates can only be a matter of conjecture, but sexual contact with a member of the opposite sex, if discovered, would be enough to result in excommunication.

In spite of revolutionary moves within the Catholic church to modify the celibacy laws, many priests still believe that chastity is preferable. Father McIntyre explained why he felt this way: ''One of the traditional arguments is that if a priest has a wife and family of his own to care for, he cannot devote his entire life to God and his parishioners, and I think there is a good deal of truth in this. I have been asked by several people how a priest copes with sexual desire. This is difficult to explain unless you understand the entire reasoning behind the law of celibacy, and anyway it varies from man to man. Fundamentally, I believe it is a question of faith—in God and in your duty as a priest to be 'available' to all men and women, which necessarily precludes any involvement or obsession with one in particular.

Unhealthy Obsession

"I have seen people 'thinking aloud,' wondering whether I notice that a particular girl is attractive. Of course I notice, but this does not mean I desire to take her to bed. Certainly sublimation is involved, and I believe this has led to an incredible number of good things, from the creation of beautiful art—painting, music, singing—to the greater awareness and understanding of life at all levels. You might say that a man is not fulfilled unless he has contact with a woman, but who is to say that such contact is worth more—to himself, God, and the world—than a life completely devoted to some greater cause?"

One reason we find it so hard to accept the idea of sublimation is that we are more aware of sex today than we have ever been before. It is undeniable that an increased understanding of the nature and mechanics of sex, leading to greater personal satisfaction, is a good thing. But with this increased awareness has come a preoccupation, some would say an unhealthy obsession, with sex as the cause of and answer to most of our problems.

Nevertheless, many of us practice sublimation, even if we are not always aware of doing so. The sex drive varies enormously from person to person, and men and women who are very highly sexed may through force of circumstance be unable to gratify their sexual urges all the time. When a sexual drive exists, but cannot be satisfied, it is more than likely that the person involved will "attack" some other kind of activity with unusually powerful vigor.

John, a young photographer of 28, admits that he feels sexually aroused very easily, and frequently. "Obviously I can't lay all the women I fancy. I mean I see at least half a dozen women a day I'd like to make love to, some of them very beautiful models indeed, but apart from the fact that few of them would be willing, I'd never get any work done that way!

Keystone

I think that wanting them but not being able to have them definitely makes me a better photographer. Taking pictures is like painting them: if you have a beautiful, desirable subject, you are obsessed by 'capturing' it—for the painter on canvas, for me in a photograph.

Neat as a Pin

"All your energies are directed to preserving the beauty you see at a particular moment and, far from spoiling your concentration or skill, feeling sexually excited lends an extra sensitivity and impetus to your performance. I definitely work better, get better results, if I desire a woman, and if I feel she is attracted to me that's even better. This sort of suppressed desire on both sides brings out the best in the model and the photographer, so I believe strongly in sublimation as a way of achieving a better standard of work."

On a more mundane level, Goldie, a young housewife, claims that she can get around the house in half the time and with much better results if she is feeling in a sexy mood. "When we haven't had time to make love in

If model and photographer find each other attractive, the result is often a picture with "sparkle."

the morning, but have wanted to badly, I usually throw myself into all the chores that normally I would spend hours over. Being turned on gives me a lot more energy and I seem to zip through work like lightning. Mind you, if I had to do without for days on end I think the reverse would happen, and the house would go to pieces, but once in a while it's a great help! We even joke about it because my husband knows that if we haven't had time to make love before he leaves the house, he'll come back to find it neat as a pin. He says we will never need a cleaning woman; all he has to do is oversleep twice a week!"

Physiologically it is easy to explain why the enforced suppression of sexual fulfillment can lead to an increase in energy, which can be diverted to other forms of activity. In an excited sexual state, the body is geared to a highly energetic performance. If sexual intercourse or some other form of sexual gratification follows, and is satisfactory, the normal result is that the body becomes quiescent and completely relaxed.

If on the other hand there is no sexual outlet, the energy remains, however temporarily, and needs to be used up. Hence the superb photograph, or the shiny house, neither of which would have happened in quite the same way if the photographer or housewife had been able to slake their sexual appetites immediately.

Sublimation can sometimes have unhappy repercussions, however. Where it becomes a way of life, where the sex drive is constantly rechanneled in order to achieve a better performance in another field, the natural expression of sexuality can be thwarted—or may even become impossible altogether.

Mary was engaged to Ian for two years before she finally decided to break it off, "not because I didn't love him any more but because I could not accept his attitude to our sex life. He rowed for a famous club and was very good, I know, but the rigorous training—at least that's what he maintained—meant that we went without sex for nights on end, weeks sometimes when he was preparing for a very important event. He reckoned that having sex reduced his performance the following day and that he needed every ounce of strength and energy to give his best efforts. It wasn't for lack of interest—he was a very passionate man—and when we did have sex it was usually marvelous, but it just wasn't often enough.

Difficult Choice

"Sometimes in the rowing season I used to go nearly out of my mind. He was loving and friendly, but shied off any real sexual contact as though I were diseased. Some of his friends held similar views, but not all. At least one boy, who also rowed, told Ian that he would lose me if he didn't pay more attention to me. I suppose my frustration must have been showing pretty badly at the time. The awful thing is that I never wanted him to give up rowing—I knew he loved everything about it and was good—but in the end I had to make him choose between me and rowing. He wouldn't make a decision, saying he could keep both. He made me feel like a sex maniac because I said this enforced celibacy was driving me crazy. He was very upset when I broke off the engagement, but he's still rowing like mad, though I know he hasn't had a regular girlfriend since."

Ian's sublimation was a conscious process in some ways, since he believed that withholding and rechanneling his sex drive would actually improve his performance as an oarsman, and his coach and many colleagues concurred with him. Inasmuch as he *was* aware of the redirection of his desire, it could be argued that he was not practicing sublimation, but some psychologists believe that the process does not have to be entirely an unconscious one, but may be in part pragmatic.

True sublimation, however, has, by definition, to be an unconscious process. It could be argued, in fact many art historians and music critics have substantiated the theory, that some of the greatest paintings and musical compositions are the indirect results of sublimation, with the vital component of genius, of course. If all the great masters had had comfortable lives with "normal," fulfilling sex lives, the world's artistic heritage would probably have been greatly diminished. The Brontë sisters, for example, created not only as a result of sensitivity, imagination, and talent, but also because they were sexually frustrated. *Jane Eyre* is a classic example of sublimation, of one girl's hopes and desires of the real world transmuted into a superb work of fiction. Tchaikovsky also, who had a tortured sexual nature which included both incestuous and homosexual leanings, practiced sublimation, creating beautiful, agonized music from his genius and his troubled, unfulfilled sexuality.

In modern life a number of apparently normal activities bear the stigma of sublimation. Driving a powerful sports car, for instance, especially if done by a man whose sex life is disappointing, could be classed as sublimation, as a doctor specializing in behavioral problems observed. "Not all men who drive big, fast cars are sublimating; to say that would be ridiculous. But for the man with sexual difficulties, driving such a car could be a way of using up the sexual energy which has no satisfactory outlet. Aggression is a vital component of sex, and a man or woman who is sexually frustrated will most probably have a good deal of aggression to cope with.

"Football even, which would seem a perfectly innocuous sport, can be the vehicle for sublimation. Rita, a football player's wife who came to see me, swore that her sex life would

The film *The Music Lovers* showed how Tchaikovsky sublimated his incestuous and homosexual feelings into creating beautiful music.

be better 'if all my husband's skill and energies were directed at me and not at that awful ball.' And though the average football enthusiast would throw up his hands in horror at the suggestion, I believe that there is more to the hugging and back-slapping that happens after scoring than simply straightforward pleasure at the achievement.

All Work and No Play

"Even the violence of some football fans, particularly the young ones, can be seen as a kind of sublimation; I suspect that if many of the young hooligans who wreck trains and stadiums and who regularly get involved in physical brawling had satisfactory outlets for their sexual desires, they would on the whole be less inclined to this kind of violence. It is only a theory, and of course many other personal and social factors are involved; but it is a theory which a number of psychologists and sociologists are investigating."

"All work and no play makes Jack a dull boy" is a well-known cliché. But the person who is unable to stop working may not just be dull; he may also, in fact, very probably, be forced to sublimate his sexual desires. It is not uncommon for people who have unhappy or frustrating sex lives to spend more and more time at work, not because they want to but because in so doing they avoid confrontation with their sexuality.

Hilary, whose marriage has been rocky for three years now, explained that it was her fault that her husband was hardly ever at home, although she felt powerless to rectify the situation. "Three years ago he discovered that I was having an affair with his boss. His immediate reaction was to leave me, which he did for two weeks. Then he came back and said it would be stupid to wreck our home and the children's lives because of this one incident. I knew he was terribly broken up about it, but I hoped that in time he would forget.

"He started to stay at work for a couple of hours in the evening, then he began to go in early in the mornings, and now he often spends all day and all night there. At first I thought it must be another woman, so I checked on him—I used to phone up at odd hours, and even dropped in on him. He was always alone, working, and even his colleagues told me to stop him from working so hard or he would have a nervous breakdown. On the contrary, he has had four promotions in the past three years and is

now number three in the firm. We have made love only six or seven times in the last three years; it isn't that he doesn't still want to, I know, but my affair seems to have dealt him a blow he can't recover from.

"Working the way he does is total sublimation. He has had some brilliant successes, done things which three years ago he wouldn't even have dreamed of, and I'm convinced that it's because all his energies and desires are channeled into one thing—his work. He is a stranger to the children now, and I know he regrets this, but it's as though he's possessed by a demon and just can't stop."

When sublimation is as total as this, it is doubtful whether the person concerned will be able to return to a life of normal sexual activity unless some outside circumstance powerful enough to change his way of life occurs, or unless he becomes aware of what he is doing and has a genuine desire to change the pattern. The interesting, though on a personal level tragic, aspect of his sublimation is that it reinforces the belief that a rechanneled sex drive can produce excellence in the occupation to which all energy has been diverted, be it writing a symphony or designing a house. It is normally assumed that it is only the happy, whole man who is capable of producing his best work, but there is more than enough evidence to suggest that the thwarted man may also manage to achieve excellent results.

Mixed Feelings

Sublimation does not have to be total, nor permanent. It may even be "used" to enhance a situation. One well-known novelist, who writes, and publishes, one best-selling novel every year, uses sublimation as a positive force from the moment he first sits down at his typewriter until his book is finished, which may take anything from three weeks to three months. "There is usually a slow buildup before I start writing the book, and during this period I may be morose, retiring, or downright aggressive. Then the moment occurs when I have to begin to write. After this *all* my energies center on the book, and only the book.

"My wife says she both dreads and welcomes this moment: dreads it because it is the end of real communication, whether emotional or sexual, until I've finished, and welcomes it because I've been behaving in an outlandish way for weeks beforehand and she wants 'to get the show

Writers may use sublimation as a positive force, directing their sexual energy into creative work to bring a chapter to life.

on the road.' When I've started the book there is literally no time or energy for anything else. If I have to describe a sex scene, for example, I can only do it when I'm keyed up myself, feeling positively horny as I write the chapter. Otherwise I can't write convincingly.

"If I were to do the obvious thing and go and make love to my wife, that section of the book would die, because in trying to capture the desire on paper, without actually living it, I can express sexuality, but if I'd just fulfilled it, there would be no impetus. That's sublimation as far as I'm concerned: getting all my thoughts, needs and desires down on paper rather than acting them out."

For this writer sublimation is a tool, not a way of life. His rechanneling results in a keener awareness, an enhanced performance. But at the point where this performance becomes the only reason for his existence, where sublimation occurs at all levels, it threatens the quality of his life, no matter what heights his diverted drives have helped him achieve, and he becomes a victim of external pressures which stifle the development of his full capacities.

Lessons in love

It's supposed to come naturally, but enjoying sex is something some of us have to work at.

Sex is only one part of a full relationship. A man and a woman in love and sharing their life together, whether married or not, enjoy each other's company and support in many ways. Many of the rewards of marriage have little direct connection with a couple's love-making—establishing a home together, raising children, building up a network of friends and relatives, helping each other through emotional or work crises and carrying through the long-term involvements of marriage.

Stresses and Strains

Love-making, however, can set the whole tone of the relationship. The couple who get on well in bed are communicating happily on at least one level and this has a happy effect on everything they do together. Problems may still exist but at least the partners will not lose touch with each other. But when the couple's sexual involvement is plagued with troubles, the resulting tensions and misunderstandings can affect every aspect of their relationship. A marriage can survive despite these problems—they settle for other rewards—but there is always a danger that it will fall apart. In this situation sexual therapy offers a couple the hope of finding sexual fulfillment and of reestablishing their marriage on a firm basis.

The first stage is recognizing that there is a source of conflict within the relationship—and that help from outsiders can be useful. One difficulty is that the couple themselves may not realize that their sexual disharmony is disturbing other areas of their life. And they may not know where to turn for help and advice.

Where the sexual failures are closely interlinked with the general strains of marriage, then friends, relatives and even colleagues at work may ease the burden almost without knowing they have become involved. One common situation comes when a young couple have a baby. The husband may still be working long hours to establish himself in a job; the wife, lacking any real guidance, expends vast amounts

Even minor sexual difficulties often seem insurmountable to a young and inexperienced person.

of energy on attempting to keep the house tidy and cope with the baby. Exhaustion sets in, love-making suffers and possibly ceases. Sexual frustration stretches the couple's nerves and begins to turn minor upsets into major quarrels.

Because the signs of strain are so obvious to outsiders, advice and help may be proffered unasked for. Colleagues may suggest to the husband that he shed some of his work load; one of the grandmothers may offer to take care of the baby for two weeks to give the couple the chance to take a vacation and reestablish the sexual side of their relationship. A break such as this—so long as the couple take the opportunity to assess what is happening to them—may be all that is needed to banish any sexual troubles since these are a symptom, rather than a cause, of difficulties.

Situations where problems revolve more directly around sexual conflicts may still respond to simple advice from easily accessible professional contacts such as the family doctor, the staff of a birth control clinic, or a marriage guidance counselor. Where misconceptions and anxiety are all that lie behind sexual difficulties then reassurance and straightforward instruction may be all that are needed.

Straight Talking

Many young couples have little direct knowledge of sexual matters and, especially during the early period of adjustment to each other, may become confused about just how they should approach love-making and what they should expect from it. Dissipating this confusion requires straight talking by someone knowledgeable about sexual matters rather than the half-embarrassed mumbles of acquaintances.

Several colleges in the United States and elsewhere have established centers where advice about sexual problems is readily available—backing this up with pamphlets such as *Elephants and Butterflies* from the University of North Carolina and *Sex is Never an Emergency* from the University of Pennsylvania. No one functions well in any sphere—physical, intellectual, social, or emotional—

when troubled by sexual anxieties, and these counseling centers, together with others open to non-students, can be of great help. Much of their activity revolves around providing contraceptive advice and assuaging young people's feelings of guilt about masturbation or sexual intercourse itself. But they go far further with help for young men complaining of impotence or premature ejaculation or young women who fear they might be frigid.

Friction or Feeling

Once again, advice and reassurance may be all that is necessary. Early sexual contacts can be fraught with anxiety. Commenting on just how common some experience of impotence or premature ejaculation is can stop a young man thinking that he alone among his fellows is sexually abnormal; explaining the nature of female sexual responses helps a young woman understand why she has not yet reached orgasm with her boyfriend; contraceptive advice takes away the inhibiting fear of pregnancy. And above all, the detached outsider can point out the difference between friction and feeling: under the frenetic conditions of one-night stands, of searching for a personal identity amid shifting concepts of what a rewarding relationship might be, sex is not as fulfilling as it might be in a more stable and secure situation.

When the problems are more deeply engrained, then more specialized professional help may be needed. Talk and advice can go only so far. The doctor, counselor, religious advisor or even lawyer who first sees one of the partners—the woman alone makes the initial move in the majority of cases; only about one in ten times do the couple appear together—may, for example, suggest psychiatric care. Where one or both partners is suffering from depression, anxiety or some other mental illness, love-making can become perfunctory and this further upsets the couple. Drug treatment or other forms of psychotherapy which alleviate the psychological disturbance ultimately may restore normal sexual functioning as part of a general return to mental well-being.

Therapy which aims directly at relieving symptoms of sexual failure is, however, becoming increasingly common. The reasons for this have much to do with the recommendations of Dr. William H. Masters and Virginia E. Johnson which resulted from their researches into human sexuality. Over a decade of research at the Reproductive Biology Foundation, St. Louis, Missouri, provided the material for their book *Human Sexual Response*, published in 1966. *Human Sexual Inadequacy*, which followed in 1970, describes their innovative clinical work and defines their attitude towards sexual dysfunction. Masters and Johnson have themselves trained therapeutic teams, others follow their guidelines, and many therapists subscribe to their basic viewpoint.

Sexual functioning, they believe, is so important to the well-being of the personality that restoring it is of prime importance. Treating sexual dysfunction directly—instead of as an adjunct to a general therapeutic program—sidesteps the psychological problems that sexual difficulties themselves produce. But they stress the importance of treating sexual dys-

function within the context of a couple's relationship and life-style. Additional therapy and counseling programs aimed at dealing with other aspects of the couple's psychological and social problems may well be necessary, but Masters and Johnson suggest that in many cases the restoration of a full and rewarding sex life can be so beneficial that the couple find they are emotionally strong enough to cope themselves with problems that previously appeared insurmountable. Masters and Johnson estimate that as many as 50 percent of married couples are afflicted by sexual problems and that many of these could be helped by some form of therapeutic program.

Rocky Relationship

Masters and Johnson telescope their therapeutic program into two weeks of night and day activity at their clinic facilities; other programs may be spread over weeks or months with visits to the therapist interspersed with controlled sexual expression and satisfaction, while another group of therapists supplements guided sexual exploration with drugs or hypnosis.

Masters and Johnson, pioneers in the field of sex therapy, use wooden dolls in counseling sessions to show couples how to stimulate and explore each other sexually.

But virtually all sex therapy programs have a common underlying structure.

The early stages involve an exploration of the psychiatric, social, and medical background of the person or couple seeking treatment. Any program aimed directly at overcoming sexual dysfunction requires the backing of counseling sessions aimed at reducing psychological and marital stresses that are involved with sexual failure, together with a medical examination to make sure that physical factors such as undiagnosed diabetes are not involved.

Exploration of specifically sexual problems follows. In the vast majority of cases these fall into the areas of male impotence and premature ejaculation and female lack of sexual response and difficulty in attaining orgasm. Talking about the individual's problems in a calm and sympathetic way sets the tone for the treatment that follows. Often this is the first time that the sufferer has been able to discuss sexual matters openly and in an adult fashion.

The therapist will be careful to avoid apportioning blame or hinting at personal inadequacy: one of the aims of therapy is to stop the kind of self-defeating recrimination that can plague a rocky relationship. Masters and Johnson's program uses a team of therapists, one male and the other female. At this stage the male therapist talks to the husband, the female to the wife, followed later by four-sided discussions. This arrangement avoids the problems that can arise if one partner feels a single therapist is siding with the other partner. The two therapists continue to supervise and offer guidance and analysis throughout the program.

With the problem areas now fully identified, some therapists will take the sufferer on a "trip into the past." By searching out and revealing the

Half of all married couples have sexual problems: therapy could help in the majority of cases.

fears, anxieties, and earlier sexual failures that have contributed to the present dysfunction, the therapist hopes to give the sufferer insight into his condition and to pave the way for a more fulfilling sexual relationship.

In one mode of therapy, particularly when the sufferer is single or is undertaking therapy separately from his partner, the therapist will give relaxant drugs or use hypnosis to produce an equivalent relaxed state, and then talk the patient through an imaginary version of the disquieting sexual act. Over several sessions of "imaginary love-making" the sufferer hopefully comes to terms with his or her anxieties and, with the help of the therapist, can transfer this newfound confidence to a real sexual encounter.

Surrogate Partners

Many therapists prefer to consult with both partners in a relationship. They believe the object is to restore full sexual functioning to both partners within the context of their ongoing involvement. Where therapists are following the Masters and Johnson

guidelines, they will attempt to alleviate the couple's sexual dysfunction by leading them through a guided program of shared sexual exploration and stimulation, aimed at destroying the ingrained reflexes that prevent full sexual functioning, and substituting responses that lead to fulfillment.

Sometimes when a single person is being treated the therapists may arrange for a surrogate partner (as Masters and Johnson have done), a volunteer whose sexuality is firmly based and who leads the sufferer through sexual exercises that ultimately lead to full intercourse.

Some therapists will even have sexual relations with certain people they treat to demonstrate to the patients that their physical sexual functioning is normal, but this can have explosive results if the patients invest their emotional energy in the therapist instead of seeking to strengthen an ordinary relationship.

The main aim of these "sensate focusing" programs is to instill sexual habits and attitudes towards love-making that will build into a

continuing fulfilling sexual life. One of the most important aspects is educating the partners in what Masters and Johnson call the "give-to-get" principle. When a couple encounter sexual failure they are liable to withdraw into their own personalities, to become critical spectators of their love-making rather than participants. Teaching each partner to give pleasure to the other begins to restore their emotional participation, and the stimulation they in turn get from the partner's increased pleasure completes the process.

Source of Pleasure

Sharing the responsibilities and enjoyments of sexual stimulation is another aspect of love-making the therapist stresses. In treating a man's premature ejaculation, his partner is shown a simple technique in which, by pressing on his erect penis around the ridge of the penile glans, she can delay his urge to ejaculate. As the man nears orgasm during foreplay he tells his partner, she squeezes, and they continue foreplay until he nears orgasm again. The man realizes it is possible to postpone his orgasmic reflex with his partner's aid and eventually learns to control his ejaculation himself. As his partner finds that she, too, has a measure of control over his reactions they begin to look upon the man's erection as *theirs,* a source of pleasure for both, rather than a focus of sexual failure for him alone.

Mapping out a route that leads the partners to full and satisfying mutual physical stimulation is the final component of the therapeutic program.

More clinical forms of sexual therapy are available to people whose problems appear more directly debilitating than lack of sexual fulfillment in an otherwise rewarding relationship. A homosexual, for example, unhappily unable to come to terms with his diverse sexual inclinations, may find a behaviorist-influenced therapist prepared to help him shift his sexual focus from males to females. An unassuming sexual deviant such as a voyeur or exhibitionist may be helped towards a maturer expression of his sexuality. And in research projects among more serious sexual criminals convicted of rape or molesting young children, scientists are investigating the effects of treatments such as hormone injections in the hope that they will enable these people to control their unacceptable sexual urges.

But the greatest contribution of

Marshall Cavendish

sexual therapy comes in aiding the vast number of ordinary relationships in which some improvement in sexual functioning pays off over and over again. The happiness of newlyweds enabled to consummate their marriage after months of frustration, the extra lease on life their renewed discovery of sexual enjoyment can give a middle-aged couple, the greatly

Some couples feel embarrassed about discussing private matters with a stranger. When they can, the battle is half won.

increased effectiveness, in all aspects of life, of the young man or woman who is freed from sexual anxiety— these are the real justifications and rewards of sexual therapy.

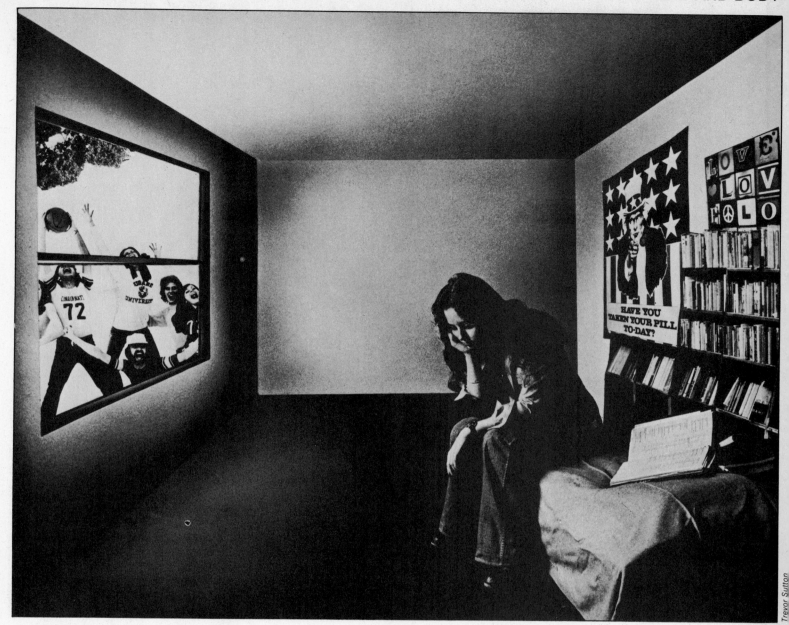

Trevor Sutton

Cloisterphobia

Life at college is a whole new ball game: neither in school nor out, neither adolescent nor mature, not yet independent but with no one but yourself to depend on. All this . . . and studying too?

The life of a student—though in many ways a privileged one—is also, for a variety of reasons, very stressful.

Firstly, it is usually during the late adolescent years that students arrive at college—a period that is inherently difficult for all young people. Establishing an adult identity and learning to form relationships with the opposite sex make heavy demands on their time and emotional energies, often accentuated by the fact that for the first time they are living away from home. This is the time when they may be

learning to cater for themselves, to cook and eat a balanced diet, to budget and manage on a small allowance, to cope with being ill or unhappy, without the cushioning comfort of their families. And on top of this, they must evolve their own way of working now that they no longer have the regimentation of school to fall back on.

Then there are the particular problems that may preoccupy the student in a new environment. He may be a foreigner, or for the first time find himself living alongside foreigners

in his own country. He may be black in a predominantly white college; *she* may be a woman in a predominantly male college, or a "mature student" who feels conspicuous among the younger majority. Whatever his worries, the student cannot afford to be "thrown" by them: for all the time the pressure is on him to do well.

One of the shocks that hits most students, once they have actually managed to reach that vaunted goal, the university, is the sheer amount of work that is demanded of them.

First they are given their timetables of daily events—lectures, seminars and tutorials, and laboratory work for the science student—and then they are confronted with a formidable list of recommended books from each of their teachers. To be presented with a whole term's reading at once is intimidating to some; to others it constitutes such an insurmountable problem that they are inclined to give up before they even begin.

But if the student is not yet daunted by the whole prospect, he may also take a look at past examination papers—to see what questions all this learning will equip him to answer—and this is the point that an attack of panic is most likely to set in.

Big Fishes

At this stage, the anxious student can get little help from his new classmates. The other students all appear to him to be terrifying, a group of sophisticated scholars who are far better read—and harder working—than himself. Before long, the camaraderie of anxiety will be established, and these paragons will reveal themselves to be as worried as he is . . . but as yet they still have their defenses up, just as he does.

Only when the student begins to own up to his apprehension can he begin to take a realistic view of his own abilities compared to the rest of his classmates. And this may come as something of a shock. At high school, the child who finally reached university standard was often the "big fish in the small pool." He was among the few who aspired to further education, and as well as walking off with most of the class prizes and accolades, he probably also received a great deal more interest and enthusiasm from his teachers than the rest of his year. Whether or not he took any particular pride in it, he was—of necessity—one of an intellectual elite.

University can come as a healthy shock to the youngster who has never yet had to stretch himself intellectually: most of the students there have reached his standard of education, are as bright, if not brighter. And he will have to readjust his view of himself, to realize that he is at the bottom of this new ladder, not the top, and must begin all over again the process of heaving himself up. There are some—those, perhaps, who have in fact reached the summit of their potential at school but who have been encouraged to struggle on to greater things—who will be daunted by this new competition, exhausted by the

idea of the steep academic climb. But to most, it acts as a challenge, a stimulus that wards off boredom.

On the other hand there are students who have never been confident of themselves, who have approached the idea of college with great trepidation, and who will gradually realize that they are more or less of the same standard as their peers and have at least a fighting chance.

During his first year at college the student's most pressing task is learning how to organize—both himself and his periods of work and relaxation. At school, the organization of the pupil's timetable is in the hands of the teachers. All he can do is try to establish disciplined habits of work, realistic levels of expectation.

Once at university, however, the student is on his own, and the amount of time and work he has to organize can be alarming. He must avoid the temptation to get away with as little studying as possible—and the (surprisingly) more common fault of spending *too much* time studying. And he must take care to cover every aspect of his course, and not to ignore the compulsory subjects that do not interest him as much as the rest.

Many colleges offer "packet" courses, combining what seem to be irrelevant subjects with the topics which the student has chosen to do. This often causes fury and frustration among students of literature, for example, who are forced to make fools of themselves in math classes, or scientists who tend to yawn their way through art history lectures.

Dreaded Chores

The philosophy of education that aims to develop the complete man, the broadly based mind, is sometimes responsible for spawning the militant activist who kicks against these imposed values. But unless he can succeed in making sensible changes to the syllabus, the student must decide to make the best of it: he has opted to do the full course when he chose the college, and, although it may seem crazy to him, bad grades in literature could kill his chances as a research chemist. Part of the process of learning to organize must be to apply himself to the dreaded chores as much as he does to the subjects he enjoys.

Tutors, if they understand the problems of the reluctant student lurking at the back of class, can help him by recommending interesting textbooks that take the drudge out of his least favorite topics, and, with luck, may even bring him to enjoy them.

Very few students ever come to enjoy the examinations, however. The specter of the final assessment, whatever shape it takes, can turn an otherwise competent, even a brilliant, student into a pathetic, shaking, incapable nervous wreck.

This is not true for all, of course: exams are hurdles that clever schoolchildren have obviously already taken in their stride. But the more urgent pressure to do well at college and the high hopes of family and friends back home can weigh on some students heavier than ever before. Most survive, but there are a few who go under. And it is vital that these few are carefully handled: the greatest intellect in the world will be of little use to a boy or girl—either at college or in the working world—if it buckles under strain. The student must learn, like everyone else, to cope with challenges and emergencies.

Stiff Upper Lip

Every student is fearful of the exam room and its implications. Most benefit by overcoming that fear for themselves, but some just cannot do so without help, perhaps even medical help. These are the people for whom the natural dread has become severe enough to warrant the title "phobia"—an irrational fear. The rearguard, stiff-upper-lip brigade of academics find it hard to reconcile themselves to the idea of psychological help, kid-glove treatment, for students who suffer like this. Often they fail to recognize that there is anything peculiar about a student who has worked himself up to a fever pitch of fear. But psychological care has reached a long arm into the universities, and is now often available to such students, once they have been identified.

Treatment for exam phobia—as with other phobias—is a process of "systematic desensitization," developed from the work of the psychiatrist Joseph Wolpe. He devised a two-part method of desensitization: first, the patient is taught how to get into a very pleasant state of relaxation; then the therapist presents to him a series of stimuli related to his phobia—either the stimuli are actually present or the patient is told to visualize them in his mind's eye. These stimuli are arranged in order of severity and only a few are presented at one session, so that over a period of time the patient builds up endurance and finds that he can stand the most terrifying of the stimuli without becoming anxious.

Applied to exam phobia, this method succeeds if a series of stimuli are

Ron Embleton

worked out beforehand with the patient's help. One stimulus might be to imagine the scene in the examination hall; another might be to write an actual exam paper.

Examination Phobia

This method often brings results, but if it is not effective—or if no such treatment has been available—there is another alternative for the student who suffers from exam phobia. If all else fails he may in special circumstances be allowed to escape the terrifying, charged atmosphere of the exam room itself, and write all his papers in a room set up by his student health service—under supervision of course, but with psychological and medical help available if he needs it.

Whether it is because of an actual phobia, or because of lack of application or talent, or even because of

sheer laziness, there are always students who fail completely—or fail in their own or their parents' eyes. Looking ahead to the expected quality of their degree, some students may, quite realistically, predict that they will be on the borderline between passing with distinction and just scraping through. The choice is then to decide whether to push themselves across that borderline or to give up the struggle. And even those who decide to make the effort—helped by their tutors, who are always more willing to help the hard workers—may eventually fail to reach their targets.

In the closed society of the college this can be a totally demoralizing and heartrending experience. All the anxiety, nervous energy, and long hours of studying for the exams, if it is followed by a huge disappointment, can bring about a complete emotional

If he's anxious about how he shapes up in class, he is doubly worried about how he looks to other students.

collapse, from which it may take months to recover. But the best way to recover is to become, as quickly as possible, a part of the world outside the university, where a completely different set of criteria applies. Outside college, the all-important matter of how exalted your degree was means little or nothing. The fact of having been to a university—and of having learned to apply your mind—means much more. Getting on with life and finding a job and a new frame of reference brings another, more pressing, sense of reality.

The hothouse atmosphere of the college is, without doubt, responsible for a great deal of neurosis among students. Many will come into the care of the university's health service suffering from the whole gamut of neurotic illness: anxiety, depression, phobia and obsessive-compulsive reaction. As in the outside world, some students are inherently more prone to neurosis than others, and for some it is not their studies that bring about their extreme anxiety but the other, equally exhausting, processes of becoming an adult.

Love School

Even for the most fortunate of students—with a secure background, a stable personality, a good brain—these years are years of difficulty. For he is seeking his role in life, building his image of himself, learning a sense of personal identity. What is more, the image he constructs depends, to a large extent, on how he thinks other people are seeing him. And the most crucial person in this respect will, to a large extent, be his lover.

Realizing that he is actually an object of love gives the student great self-confidence and increased vitality across a whole range of activities. But this crucial relationship—with someone whom he values and who values him in turn—is just where many of his problems begin.

Perhaps they should not be called problems at all: perhaps it is more realistic to allow that life *is* difficult at times, and that it is precisely in overcoming these difficulties that people grow to be adults. It is, of course a matter of degree, and it is when the problem gets too big to handle himself that the student calls out for help. There are endless love difficulties which the student may come to think of as "blighting his life," or as symptoms of all-around failure that might even drive him to think of suicide, let alone ruin his studies—the reason for his being there at all.

He may be unable to find a partner, particularly as some colleges have a distinct minority of women. (Girl students may have the opposite problem seeming to be at the center of terrible rivalry and turmoil.) He may collapse after the end of a relationship—whether he or his partner finishes the affair. He may be consumed with jealousy, or overcome with shyness. He may feel he is a complete flop with the opposite sex.

A relationship at college is apt to become intense in the extreme, perhaps because it may be the first true sexual love affair. There will be anxieties about contraception, embarrassment at lack of sexual expertise, fears about impotence, or frigidity. And there may be the trauma of an unwanted pregnancy to go through. Some students will need a great deal of counseling, for this is the time when many underlying problems will begin to emerge for the first time—hang-ups and misconceptions left over from childhood which are only now coming to the surface.

An astonishing number of young people go to the university completely unequipped to cope with the problems that the first serious love affair will bring. In the opinion of one British student health doctor, sex education at present is "hopeless, and arouses contempt": students go to college badly prepared, if prepared at all, for one of the most important facets of life there. All the more reason to use college as an opportunity for this broader form of student education, as "institutions of higher education are ideal for proper love/sex education because of the age group they serve and because their students will be future molders of opinion."

Sex Education

What are the consequences of this lack of sex knowledge which students bring to the university? Since most universities do not offer sex education the students take it upon themselves to organize, for example, lectures by "controversial" speakers—thus often causing an immediate outcry from some quarters and the condemnation of such activities as immoral and obscene.

Otherwise, there are various people who pick up the pieces, including the university health service doctors and the chaplains of the different religions. There are also organizations like the Samaritans and "Contact" who will lend an ear to a desperate voice on the other end of the telephone.

Tutors and other members of staff get a few cries for help. One very

PAF International

Not every student has problems: college can give the expanding intellect room and time to develop.

PAF International

important job that they can do is to spot the fact that a student is ill: he may have drifted imperceptibly into a mild depression and nobody has noticed it. Someone who sees a student at regular intervals, such as at weekly tutorials, may be able to detect small changes that indicate trouble.

Drug Problems

If students do develop more severe psychological illnesses, such as schizophrenia or manic depression, they may just disappear inside their lodgings, or their home, without trace. It is most important to spot these illnesses and to ensure that the student is seen by the university doctor in case they need hospital treatment.

Only too often student problems are compounded by drugs. With the vigorous action of the police in recent years, the illegal use of drugs among students has probably been reduced, but the problem is always there, lurking in the background, and it is one which can severely disturb a student's career, even his whole life.

The drugs in question are mainly cannabis and LSD, but amphetamines and opiates such as morphine and heroin are also sometimes involved. An important feature of the drug taker's world is that he is given the opportunity to join the drug "subculture" a group of fellow drug takers who may provide the student with a sense of belonging, a group of people who are, in some sense, superior to the earthbound culture outside. This superiority may rest on a quasi-mystical experience of a deeper reality with which the drug taker feels he is in contact.

Objectively, little of positive value appears to come out of the drug subculture. Moreover, any contact with even the milder drugs may be very dangerous for the impressionable student, since it opens up the possibility of moving from the innocuous cannabis to the dangerous LSD, the very dangerous amphetamines and the deadly opiates—morphine and heroin.

According to Anthony Ryle, in his book *Student Casualties*, about 30 percent of all students have at least one experience of drug taking, but only about 10 percent take any drug regularly—and often it is no more

Much of the education that goes on at college—learning to form the first mature relationships with both lovers and friends—happens outside the classroom.

dangerous than cannabis or hash.

However, a small number of students go downhill and become addicted to the opiates. They are then likely to fail academically and to run into troubles with the police. The treatment of patients such as these is extremely difficult and their outlook is very depressing indeed.

The benefits other students have at college are enormous—but so are their needs. They are exposed to very many stresses and can easily make a series of well-recognized errors. At one time or another most students will need a helping hand—someone who really understands their problems. University student health services have collected a great deal of valuable information about the various hazards and pitfalls of the student life: by plowing back all their experience they will be able to contribute a great deal to the happiness of students.

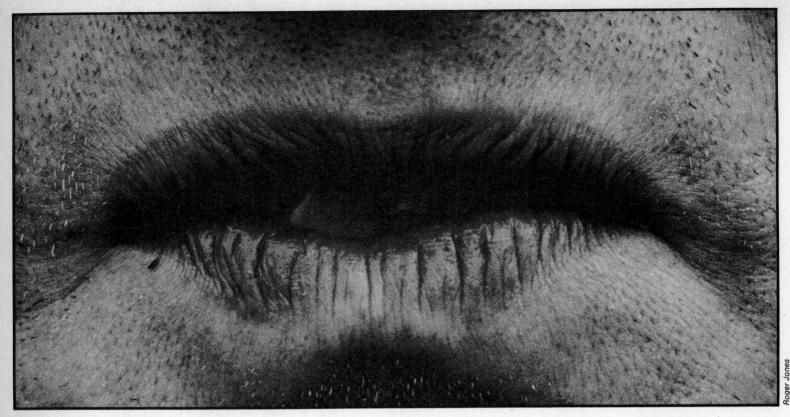

Roger Jones

Deleted expletive

The decline and virtual fall of the naughty word has been one of the many side effects of the permissive society. The naughtiest words of previous decades are widely established in our daily vocabulary with the result that their naughtiness is nullified.

Historically speaking, there were three separate elements comprising the value of the naughty word. It was risqué, it could shock, and it provided a useful safety valve: a verbal outburst was often more practical than a physical one.

Swear Box

The risk of using obscene language or swearing reached a peak in Scotland in 1645, when the Scottish Parliament made cursing a crime punishable by death. The British Profane Oaths Act of 1745 contented itself with fines that varied according to the offender's social standing. Laborers, soldiers or sailors were fined a shilling, anyone who was beneath the rank of gentleman, two shillings, and those above it, five shillings. Insolvent offenders were awarded ten days hard labor instead. The potential financial

disadvantage was increased by the fact that a man who went in for a succession of oaths paid for each one separately. Presumably to avoid this penalty, the crafty cursers evolved a cunning system of composites, such as "Deviltakethefathersonand holyghost." For some reason, the act did not apply to women, who were probably considered to be above such base forms of expression.

Times have changed. In Britain in the autumn of 1965, the literary director of the National Theatre, Kenneth Tynan, dared to use a four-letter word on a BBC television program. There was an instant and outraged uproar. A motion was even proposed in the House of Commons asking for Tynan's dismissal. At this point, the outcry was exposed to ridicule when a more liberal MP suggested that Tynan should not be dismissed until the Minister of Defense had discharged from the armed forces all soldiers, sailors, and airmen who had used the forbidden four-letter word during the previous five years.

Nowadays, the risk of a private individual being prosecuted for the use

of obscene or blasphemous language is negligible. The danger element in the use of naughty words may be extinct, but the shock and safety qualities are still with us. There is widespread agreement on the psychological benefits of swearing. Coleridge referred to it as "so much superfluous steam that would endanger the vessel if it were retained," while Tristram Shandy's father informs us, "I swear on until I find myself easy."

Vengeful Verbosity

Swearing of this sort is very closely allied to verbal threat, and one of its intriguing characteristics is that we swear or threaten far more than it would be practical to fulfill. "I'd like to tear him limb from limb" is a threat which would require greater strength than most of us are endowed with, and would be messily unpleasant anyway. The heights of vengeful verbal destructiveness that we reach so easily tend to exceed the degree of damage we are really prepared to do.

Although letting off steam by swearing may alleviate the strain on a nation's hospital services, the shock-

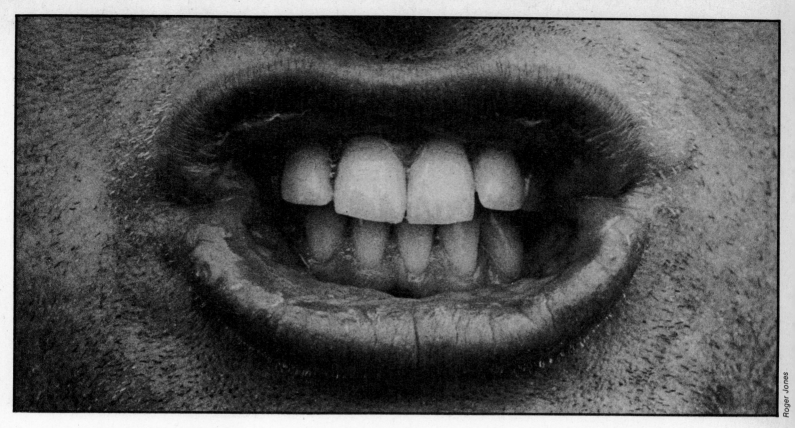

Roger Jones

ing aspects of naughty words fulfill an equally important personal function. If some insensitive human being irritates us, we may be too cowardly or too frightened of the terrible results of our own strength to resort to physical violence. So we rely on swearing, which relieves our own tensions and, hopefully, upsets the opposition.

Term of Endearment

Our aggressive verbal currency is at the moment sadly devalued. Of the two principal kinds of swearing, the religious is dead and the secular is difficult. The religious type is defunct because the majority of people today are utterly unimpressed by Father, Son, Holy Ghost, and the whole host of saints who once provided such varied inspiration for swearing. The secular form is difficult because it is almost impossible, except for someone blessed with a diseased or completely depraved imagination to conjure up anything that will remotely shock anyone any more. Swearing is inevitably subject to social considerations: to succeed in being supremely abusive, a swearer needs detailed knowledge of his opponent's views.

"Bastard" used to be an unforgivable term of abuse among the lower classes, for whom illegitimacy constituted a serious sin. In the aristocracy, however, there was far greater tolerance of bastards, who often had noble or even royal blood in their veins. Under the title of "natural sons and daughters," they often enjoyed more privileges than their kin born on the right side of the blanket.

On the other hand, "bugger" was a pointless insult among the lower classes, who were less prone to homosexual practices. Dr. Johnson even defined the word as "a term of endearment among sailors." But among the upper classes, who were more conscious of the stigma of sexual deviation, the accusation was an outrage. If Oscar Wilde had merely been called a bastard, no one would have minded.

There was also an extremely strong taboo on mentioning the private parts of the body. This could reach ludicrous extremes, as in the case of a wounded soldier who, when asked by a visitor where he had been shot, could only reply, "I'm so sorry, ma'am, I don't know; I never learned Latin."

Equally strong was the lavatory taboo. This is not particularly surprising in itself, since not even the most permissive campaigner can claim great aesthetic qualities for defecation. What is difficult to understand is the extraordinary amount of territory this unnatural modesty obscured. Not only was it considered obscene for a man to show a woman the way to the lavatory, but even man to man, or woman to woman, an evasive phrase had to be used, "Would you care to wash your hands?" or "Have you seen the geography of the house?" were suitable substitutes. Intimate friends would not even consent to notice each other if one of them was emerging from the lavatory or entering it and, if this was the first meeting of the day, would greet each other half a minute later on untaboo ground with every pretense of novelty and surprise.

The readiness with which the term "shit" is bandied about in the permissive society is indicative of the erosion of this traditional area of reserve. The same is true of the more sexual terms of abuse. Indeed, because previous values have been turned upside down, the more excessive the accusation of sexual deviation, the more flattering it is to be accused. "Son of a bitch" has been common usage for several decades as the tale of an American tourist, Mrs. Beech, who was staying in Paris after the war, related. An elderly Frenchman who was introduced to her greeted her cordially, "Ah, Misses Beech, you are one of ze noble muzzaires who gave so many sons to ze war."

Mentally Ill

Possibly the only area where taboos remain strong enough to provide valuable ammunition for obscene swearing is that of incest: hence the popular epithet which accuses a man of having sexual intercourse with his mother. The principal problem faced by swearing in a society overwhelmed by frankness is whether it should attempt to go even further or whether it should take a different course. For instance, a most effective insult could be to call someone a virgin!

Apart from its use in aggressive swearing, obscene language is also prevalent among the mentally ill. Some emotionally disturbed cases tend persistently to utter obscenities. This is associated with their lack of respect for other people, which is in turn bound up with their own loss of self-respect. Freud, with his characteristic determination, if not accuracy, decided that obscene words represented attempts to force the hearer to picture the content of the word. Thus obscenity, in the presence of a woman, may be a form of verbal rape.

According to some sources, there are men who insist that their women indulge in obscene language before or during sexual intercourse. As one lady put it, "I not only have to do it, but say it as well." There are also some men who enjoy talking to their partners in obscene language. This is presumably a kind of decadent antithesis to the men and women who like to be told how much they are loved during sexual intercourse.

Naughty verbal obscenities are not confined to swearing and sexual stimulation—they can also be entertaining. Evidence of our delight in naughty words is provided by the enduring popularity of the entire tradition of bawdy literature and dirty jokes. The father of English literature, Chaucer himself, knew how to turn a smutty line or two. In *The Merchant's Tale,* we find an interesting and highly gymnastic passage (modern translation):

. . . and with a spring she thence
—Ladies, I beg you not to take
  offense
I can't embellish, I'm a simple man—
Went up into the tree, and Damian
Pulled up her smock at once and in
  he thrust.

Likewise in *The Miller's Tale:*
Now Nicholas had risen for a piss
And thought he could improve upon
  the jape
And make him kiss his arse ere he
  escape,
And opening the window with a jerk,
Stuck out his arse, a handsome
  piece of work,
Buttocks and all, as far as to the
  haunch.
Said Absalom, all set to make a
  launch,
"Speak, pretty bird, I know not
  where thou art!"

This Nicholas at once let fly a
  fart
As loud as if it were a thunder-
  clap.
He was near blinded by the blast,
  poor chap,
But his hot iron was ready; with
  a thump
He smote him in the middle of the
  rump.

The Elizabethans were particularly fond of naughty puns and Shakespeare was no exception. Hamlet's wordplay on "country matters" is typical, as is his play on "nunnery" with its Old English meaning of whorehouse.

Bawdy Books

What was considered acceptable in literature has, like everything else, varied with the age. The process seems to be one of extremes, pivoting from an age in which excessive sanctity prevails to one where nothing is sacred. Bawdy literature did not do too well under the puritans but the succeeding age, as exemplified by Fielding in *Tom Jones,* took a delight in every kind of naughty situation.

To shock others some people rely very heavily on four-letter words.

Rob Matheson

an industrial company. Expenditure on equipment installed to reduce pollution may be entered up, but the cost incurred in other ways is "invisible," incalculable, and far more considerable. Now, in the end, it is that company which pays the bill; the expense becomes an additional production cost which is passed onto the consumer in higher prices. Similarly if a government takes steps to control pollution which involve huge public expenditure it is the taxpayer who has to fork out.

Among the greatest assets of any industry, even if not so tangible as financial or capital investment, are the health and welfare of its work force, a high degree of productivity and co-operation, good working conditions, a low rate of absenteeism, an agreeable environment, and a pleasant community life for its workers and their families. Pollution can eliminate all these advantages at a stroke.

The story of the community rising up against its industrial overlords for destroying the valley to which they once promised prosperity is as old as the hills they have scarred and blackened. Their chimney stacks belch forth smoke, soot, corrosive acids, toxic fumes, and grime which rain down over a much wider area sullying people, their clothes, their homes, their gardens, their property. Meanwhile the surrounding countryside becomes pockmarked with dumping sites for industrial waste, and the rivers and streams which once flowed through the playgrounds of the local community become conveyor belts for rotting refuse and stinking effluent.

The workers fall prey to industrial diseases from the lifelong intake of contaminated air and water, or they become psychologically demoralized. They either cannot work or do so without enthusiasm. The people and the industry they serve, which in turn serves them by providing employment, become sworn enemies. If all this could be totted up and seen in terms of a financial liability to be entered on a company balance sheet as losses, pollution would be seen for what it is.

Safe Limit

The Council of Environmental Quality estimates that lost working days take $6 billion a year out of the economy of the United States. The loss to industry is one thing, but the cost to the individual absentee is proportionally greater. There are his lost earnings to be considered as well as his having to meet doctors' or hospital bills. Even where he is taken care of by the state, or compensated or reimbursed by some other enterprise, it does not mean that his health will necessarily be reinstated.

Sadly, pollution is here to stay. We have accepted not only that it is inevitable, but that a certain amount is permissible. We, and other living things on this planet, are sufficiently resilient and adaptable to resist small doses of contamination without suffering undue harm. But where do we draw the line? We can fix limits to the amount of pollution acceptable—the safe limit of the nitrate content of water set by the World Health Organization at 100 parts per million.

But establishing such thresholds is fraught with complications. The susceptibility to contamination of any sort varies from person to person. And while we are simultaneously exposed to a variety of forms of pollution—in the air from toxic gasses and radiation, in our water supplies, and in the food we eat—our bodies may be able to cope with a certain amount of one or another kind of poison but may not be able to overcome the cumulative

Our beaches are now tarred and feathered as well as littered.

Camera Press

effect. The same goes for the resistance of the natural environment to waste matter. Moreover, we never know precisely when and where the agents of contamination are present and in what concentrations.

The only way to be absolutely sure of effectively protecting ourselves and our environment is to set the limit of pollution permissible as low as possible—that is to say, none at all. But this means no industry, no technology, no modern techniques in agriculture; it means outlawing the motor car and all forms of speedy transport; it means evacuating the cities and dispersing their populations in the hills from which they came.

Although some people would say that these would be the most "progressive" steps man could take, they are clearly impracticable, and even the most stentorian cry of "Stop the World!" is unlikely to be heeded. Backtracking is far more difficult than forging ahead. So we have to find ways of scaling down pollution which our existing industrial and domestic systems create, reorganize our economic arrangements so that unnecessary pollution can be eliminated, devise new methods of disposing of solid, liquid, and gaseous wastes, or else rely on science to come up with new sources of power and means of production which do not have pollutant by-products.

Heavy Penalties

These aims are being vigorously pursued, but meanwhile we have to deal with the present emergency. This has arisen because up until recently the natural environment has been regarded as a free repository for human and industrial waste. Large-scale polluters have not always been impressed by the argument that he who makes the mess should clear it up, for to do so would be, in economic terms, a waste of money, manpower, time, and energy. Although, as we have seen, the effects of pollution rebound directly onto the industries which perpetrate it, even that has not proved sufficient incentive to prompt countermeasures. Moral obligation has therefore to be reinforced by law.

But legislation is always behind the times, often enacted long after the damage has been done. With pollution the damage often takes years to make itself felt, and the law might take even longer to catch up. Even now companies can pollute the environment in any number of ways, imposing intolerable discomfort and hardship on the neighboring community and its

Camera Press

wildlife, and still be operating within the letter of the law. Legal enforcement always involves public expenditure which falls upon the taxpaying citizen, who also has to pay in higher prices for any measures the polluter is himself constrained to take.

Among the most successful anti-pollution laws was Britain's 1956 Clean Air Act, which established smokeless zones in which it is now forbidden to burn untreated coal. This significantly reduced the amount of sulphur dioxide being released into the air in the cities. There have been other such statutes, but governments and municipal authorities can exercise further control of airborne pollution by setting limits on the amount of this and other gases like oxides of nitrogen passing into the atmosphere, and of solid and liquid effluent passing into waterways. Enforced by roving inspectors who ensure that the thresholds are not exceeded, such laws would carry heavy penalties in the form of bans and prohibitive fines, so that polluters are regarded not just as antisocial but as lawless. The penal system must be harsh so that it is in the long run

Nonreturnable bottles are returned to an offending manufacturer.

cheaper to refrain from polluting.

Because pollution is not just a local matter, affecting the immediate environs, but enters air and waterways, finding its way far afield, there is increasing demand for international legislation to minimize its effects. This is particularly urgent in the case of oil pollution of coastal and ocean waters. The *Torrey Canyon* disaster, which wrought havoc on the beaches of Britain, has underlined the need for this. Britain herself, with the Prevention of Oil Pollution Act, has set the maximum penalty for oil pollution at £50,000 and in 1973 won 43 cases.

So legal sanctions against polluters, while imperative, are not as effective as they might be. Even imposing charges on polluting industries for the privilege of discharging wastes into the environment—thereby shattering the illusion that dumping is free—does not strike at the heart of the problem. Like legislation, such charges would reduce the amount of indiscriminate pollution and cause potential despoilers to tread warily.

Yet they do nothing to change the industrial, domestic, or agricultural processes where it originates, nor do they impose any restraints on the demands of the consumer. In this respect action is required from the industries themselves and from the professional bodies which regulate their activities. For instance, the Soap and Detergent Association sets standards for the chemical content of all brands under its aegis to minimize the dispersal of phosphates and nitrates into domestic disposal systems and water supplies, while overseeing research into less harmful ingredients.

Alternative Energy

Science and technology have been examining thermal, tidal, and solar power as alternative sources of energy. It will be a long time before they can be tapped for industrial use or domestic consumption, or adapted for transport. If and when this happens, many of our pollution worries will be over, but they will eliminate only the power generation stage of the pollution process. That still leaves us with the emissions and waste materials of the production processes themselves and the aftermath of consumption. While it is easy to conceive of other means of power and disposal, it is harder to envisage alternative sources of food. Assuming we shall continue to eat what we have always eaten, the land will have to produce more than ever to feed the swelling populations of the world, which implies increasing reliance on chemicals.

The nonpolluting alternative to chemical treatment of the land is biological control. Nobody is suggesting that chemicals should be banned altogether, considering particularly that in parts of Asia 25 percent of a harvest goes to feed predators rather than people. But there have been spectacular failures of pest control which have cast doubt on the validity of chemical methods. Perhaps the most notable of these was the attempt to eradicate the fire ant from the south eastern states of America. Twenty million acres were sprayed with heptachlor, which, so it was later found, was transformed into a toxic derivative which turned up in meat and milk. Not only was wild life destroyed as a result of this scorched earth program, the fire ant still flourished and spread to other states.

Contrast this fiasco with the successful assault on the screwworm fly, a pest harmful to livestock, which has been annihilated without a drop of chemical being sprayed. A massive program was launched to sterilize the

male of the species. As the female mates only once, the rate of reproduction could be abated by releasing the sterile males into infested areas. It worked, and the pest was eventually exterminated. This kind of biological control, as opposed to chemical control, calls for far greater ingenuity and imagination and takes longer to show results, but in the long run it may prove safer than the pesticide sprays that have been in use.

Introducing predators or viruses to attack specific pests is another form of biological control. This demands a comprehensive working knowledge of the cycle of nature. Like pesticides, such action introduces something new into the natural system, and, by wiping out a whole species, removes a link from the food chain. But unlike chemicals, there is no residue of poison destroying other life in its wake, impregnating the land, and seeping out into waterways—and all that inevitably ensues. The fail-safe method of biological control, however, is to develop strains of crops and livestock resistant to pests, disease, and contamination.

Financial Incentive

But how can we deal with the increasing rate of waste disposal? In the absence of nonpolluting methods, the answer seems to be to throw away less. As long as producers find it cheaper and more efficient to use new materials rather than reuse old ones, the rate of disposal will continue to rise, the amount of discarded matter will just go on accumulating, and there will be no financial incentive for anyone to reverse the trend. The incentive will eventually be sheer survival, for the rapid depletion of world resources and the sudden shortage of materials will force us to adopt "waste not, want not" philosophies.

The word "recycling" is very much in vogue and is being bandied about in the highest government quarters. Recycling is particularly pertinent to the packaging industry, which produces billions of tons of containers which once emptied are useless and contribute significantly to domestic pollution that is even now overwhelming municipal refuse disposal authorities. Metal, glass, plastic, paper and countless other natural or synthetic materials are all reusable if returned to the appropriate processing plant. As it is, the bulk of these materials is dumped, burned, buried, or submerged, in most cases both needlessly and destructively.

If we even reach the point where all

serviceable material is recycled, we will have succeeded in reproducing in our technosphere a "natural cycle" similar to the one which already successfully operates in the biosphere—despite our worst efforts to disrupt it. The two worlds will then work in harmony so that technology can forge ahead without prevailing upon the environment to pick up the pieces.

Another specter—more nebulous, yet more haunting—casts a shadow over the future: even if we could reduce pollution by using new approved materials and disposal techniques to supplement our natural absorption and decomposition processes, the combined defense mechanism would be no guarantee against some drastic imbalance of nature occurring or some catastrophic breakdown or accident befalling our technology. What if a nuclear power station were unwittingly to release vast quantities of radioactivity into the environment? What if some unforeseen chemical reaction proves too powerful for industrial safety precautions? The safeguards we introduce to cover such eventualities—and the atomic energy industry is more safety conscious than most conventional undertakings—may prove inadequate. As we press on with our technological development, taking chances and ignoring the warnings of environmentalists, we will maximize production by overusing, overloading, and overexerting the system beyond its capacity.

In between the indiscriminate polluter and the fanatic "ecofreak" there is room for more people with scientific and technical skills coupled with good sense and compassion, whose efforts would give us some confidence that the pollution menace is facing strong opposition. The ecological and conservationist lobby is becoming more and more boisterous, and is more often drawn into consultations, while the preservation of the environment is rising higher in the scale of priorities considered by politicians, legislators, and administrators.

Technology is much more powerful than man himself, and certainly more so than the environment in its natural state. So long as it remains under man's push-button control, it can be used either to preserve and protect or to desecrate and destroy.

The human element is still the decisive factor, and the survival of life on this planet depends on whether man, its senior species, exercises the wisdom and reason with which he has been endowed or displays the abysmal folly of which he is supremely capable.

David Kinefield

What happens now?

Nothing is as sure as death, yet when a loved one dies it still leaves us in a state of shock.

The specter of the death of a loved one—a member of the family—plays a central role in the life of every individual. We have all known, or will know, death, grief and mourning.

Avoiding the Subject

The writer Suzanne Ramos describes how a friend of hers died, leaving her husband and a five-year-old son, Mark. After several weeks Mark became very depressed. He grew more and more silent. He would sit for hours just staring out of the window. He picked at his food. And then he began to refuse to go to school. His father consulted the family doctor, who referred him to Gilbert Kliman, an American child psychiatrist who specializes in helping children cope with such traumatic experiences as death, serious illness, and other crises that shake families from time to time. He was able to reassure Mark's father that the boy's reaction was not particularly unusual. The father was given concrete guidance on how to help Mark mourn the death of his mother and thus come to terms with his loss.

A recurring problem is the understandable tendency for parents to avoid the unpleasant subject of death. They say, ''There's plenty of time to worry about that later.'' But all children who lose a parent, a brother or sister, a beloved relative, or a playmate can be spared unnecessary serious emotional repercussions

Above: Time is a great healer but it can take a long while to get used to his not being around any more.

later if they have had their eyes opened to the reality of death and if it occurs, are encouraged to express their feelings at the time. If they are helped to mourn the loss they can eventually come to accept the death, although this does not always work, even with adults!

John Smith was 47 when his wife died unexpectedly after a short illness, leaving him with two children of school age. No one was concerned at first when he appeared desperately unhappy and withdrawn. In fact, people left him alone with his sorrow.

Marshall Cavendish

Marshall Cavendish

However, as time went by he remained persistently depressed and unable to work. He was referred for psychiatric help by his family doctor. It was clear that the main difficulties causing his failure to adjust to his wife's death lay in his personality. He had always been a quiet, shy man, whose only close emotional links had been with his wife—"We did everything together." He had become isolated from his family and had no friends, no one to turn to when he needed help. Consequently he had to take on the role of his dead wife—he was doing all the household chores and could not go to work because there was no one to care for the children when they came home from school. With the support of a social worker, he was gradually able to make contact with neighbors, who, as it happened, had been anxious to help but too shy to make an approach. He arranged for a young couple with children to take lodgings in his house, and he was eventually able to overcome his grief and return to work. He had lacked the practical and emotional support of friends and neighbors.

Grief, as it is used in everyday conversation, usually refers to extreme sorrow associated with loss or separation. We grieve the departure of a dear friend to another country; the child grieves when his mother leaves him in the hospital; we feel grief when we lose a loved one's affection or when we lose our illusions about him. According to the psychoanalyst George Pollock, normal grief seems to pass through three stages. First, there is a short period of intense shock when the bereaved person feels numb and unable to give full vent to his distress. This results from the disruption of the individual's psychological equilibrium—a sudden awareness that the loved one no longer exists in time and space. Luckily, this period, which may last for a few hours or even a few days, is usually a very busy time when members of the family gather around the bereaved and give him a great deal of help and support with the many purely practical problems which have to be dealt with after a death. The overwhelming task of coming to terms with the shock may not be dealt with successfully and may then result in panic; shrieking, wailing or moaning may follow, or there may be complete collapse.

The reactions in this initial phase vary in intensity according to the

Reflecting on the good times is a bittersweet sensation for the bereaved, but preserving their memory keeps the dead alive.

suddenness of the death and the amount of preparation the bereaved had beforehand. Death following chronic and prolonged illness is responded to differently from an unexpected loss. In certain predisposed individuals, Dr. Pollock reports, the shock can be great enough to precipitate a serious physical disorder. Where long anticipated, mourning reactions may occur prior to death.

Feeling of Impotence

The second stage postulated by Dr. Pollock is the "grief reaction." In *The Expression of the Emotions in Man and Animals*, Charles Darwin described the physical aspects of grief. In the early stage it is characterized by muscular hyperactivity, like hand wringing, aimless wild walking, pulling of hair and clothes. Darwin believed that this behavior indicated the impotence felt by the mourner—the feeling that he was unable to reverse the death which had occurred. These restless, frantic movements subside when he realizes and accepts that nothing can be done. Then deep despair and sorrow take over: the sufferer becomes very quiet, sits motionless or gently rocks to-and-fro, sighs deeply and becomes muscularly flaccid. All the facial features are lengthened, giving the characteristic appearance of grief. Fatigue, exhaustion, and anorexia are often part of this acute phase of grief.

As the shock phase merges into the grief stage, so numbness turns into pain. Dr. Pollock says, "The suffering ache is initially of much greater intensity than what subsequently follows in the later chronic grief phase. Accompanying this psychic pain may be the sudden screaming, yelling and other nonverbal but vocal manifestations of this grief reaction. The acute initial response later becomes the more characteristic depression. The spasmodic crying changes to tearful lamentations, and gradually verbal communications become more frequent though still accompanied by much sobbing."

Transfer of Bonds

In the stage of acute grief the bereaved may suffer from acute feelings of guilt. Could he have made the last days of the dead person more pleasant? If he had been taken to the hospital earlier, would his life have been saved? The bereaved may even go so far as to accuse himself of contributing actively to the death by neglect.

The final phase is one of slow recovery, both physical and emotional, in which the grief is slowly dissipated by renewed contact with the external world. All the shared emotional bonds are gradually transferred to other people and activities as the bereaved person rebuilds a new pattern of life. It is only when new emotional bonds are established in place of the old that a person has come to terms with his grief and "filled the gap."

Freud, in his monograph "Mourning and Melancholia" (1917), compared the normal emotion of grief and its expression in mourning with the psychosis melancholia. He based this comparison upon the general picture of the two conditions as well as upon the external precipitating causes, which were the same in both cases.

According to the argument, the loss of a loved object gives rise to behavior and feelings collectively referred to as mourning; these psychological processes are always set in train by the disruption of a precious attachment. If mourning takes its normal course, the person gets over the tragedy and is capable of making a new attachment. But it might also (in people of a pathological disposition) give rise to a deep-seated depression or melancholia.

In melancholia, the symptoms are: painful dejection; loss of interest in the external world; inhibition of activity; loss of capacity to love; loss of self-esteem and hence self-reproach and delusional expectations of punishment. These are the same symptoms as in mourning, with the exception of loss of self-esteem and the expectation of punishment.

In both mourning and melancholia —according to Freud—the precipitating cause is the same: the loss of a loved object. It need not involve another human being; it may concern something which has taken the place of the loved object such as a person's freedom, his fatherland, or some ideal. Both mourning and melancholia are marked by departures from normal behavior. However, the grief of mourning is not regarded as a pathological condition: no one thinks of sending the mourner to a psychiatrist.

It is anticipated that time will cure grief, and usually people think that grief should be left alone to take its course. However, according to the eminent British researcher Dr. John Bowlby, infants and children may, in certain circumstances, react to separation from their mothers by mourning processes which predispose them to psychiatric illness in later life.

Essential Mourning

The normal processes of mourning bring about a withdrawal of emotional concern from the lost person and commonly prepare the ground for making new relationships. Psychoanalysts have emphasized that the identification of the bereaved person with the deceased is the main process involved in mourning—part of himself, an extension of his ego, has died. This theory makes it plain why working through the mourning process is essential to self-recovery.

Bowlby formulates a theory of mourning which, like Pollock's, distinguishes three main phases but has more to do with personality changes. During the first phase, the individual's attachments are still focused on the lost object, but for obvious reasons they cannot be resolved. As a result, the bereaved experiences repeated disappointment, the anxiety of persistent separation, and, insofar as he accepts reality, grief. So long as the affections and dependencies are focused on the deceased, there are strenuous and often angry efforts to recover him. The widow may strive in actuality or in her mind to retrieve her husband. She may attend spiritualist seances to get in touch; she cries for him and calls out his name. There may be outbursts of anger when she reproaches him for deserting her.

The futility of such efforts is obvious to others and sometimes to the bereaved herself, yet the efforts may continue. Dr. Bowlby believes that the seeds of much mental illness are sown in this phase. When the mourning process proceeds healthily, however, the various needs of the individual cease to focus on the dead, and the efforts to recover him stop.

Emotional Detachment

In the second stage, before the final resolution, there is a disorganization of the personality accompanied by pain and despair. In the first two stages, feelings fluctuate, often between angrily demanding and pitifully expecting the loved one to return, between a despair expressed in subdued pining and total lack of any expression. Though hope and despair may alternate for a long time, there evolves, at last, a degree of emotional detachment from the deceased.

During the third stage, the function of mourning is complete, and a new and different state has come about: a reorganization of attitudes and feelings, partly in relation to the image of the lost person, partly in connection with a new object or objects. Children show this pattern of mourning when separated early in life from their mothers. The consequences, if adequate substitute care is not provided, can be serious.

The psychiatrist Dr. Spitz made a study of 123 unselected children at a nursery for the babies of women offenders. The infants stayed in the nursery from their fourteenth day of life until the end of their first year and in a few cases until the end of their eighteenth month. All shared the same environment, care and food. When the infants were somewhere between their sixth and eighth months, their mothers were kept almost totally from them, seeing them at best once a week, whereas before the separation they had had full care of their babies and spent more time with them than is probably usual for an ordinary mother in an ordinary home.

A striking syndrome was afterwards observed in the babies. The principal symptoms were not all necessarily present at the same time, but all of them were noticeable at one point or another in the clinical picture. They were: apprehension, sadness, weeping; lack of contact, rejection of environment, withdrawal; retardation of development and reaction to stimuli, and slowness of movement; dejection, stupor, frozen immobility; loss of appetite, refusal to eat, loss of weight; and insomnia.

Added to these, they showed a facial expression which Spitz found difficult to describe, but which in an adult would indicate depression. This syndrome developed in the course of four to six weeks following the mother's removal. None of the children whose mothers had not been removed developed the syndrome.

The depression syndrome occurred only in those children who were deprived of their love object for an appreciable period during the first year of their life, although, on the other hand, not all the children whose mothers were removed developed the same syndrome. Hence, Spitz suggests, maternal separation is a necessary—but not a sufficient—cause for the development of this "anaclitic depression" syndrome.

Animal Parallel

Mourning the death of a loved one is not exclusively human behavior. Dr. Bowlby claims that the evidence, fragmentary though it is, makes it fairly certain that each of the main behavioral features alleged to be characteristic of human mourning is essentially shared with other animals. Animals also protest at the loss of a loved object and do everything in their power to seek and recover it. Frequently they become hostile and withdrawn, rejecting a potential new object; apathy and restlessness are the rule. Yet, given time and opportunity, they eventually find a new object of affection and recover.

Dr. Bowlby's theory has received support from the zoologist Konrad Lorenz in his studies of jackdaws, geese, dogs, orangutans, and chimpanzees. A greylag goose which had lost its mate at first began a frantic searching and calling. Then followed the phase of depression: the bird lacked energy, its movements were slow, its eyes seemed smaller, its feathers were loose and slightly fluffed, its head and neck were less erect, and it was noticeably less keen to fly. These bereaved geese also exhibit a disinclination for social contacts. They are generally ignored by other geese, Lorenz maintains, and "grief-stricken widows of this type are hardly ever courted by males, even if a quite considerable shortage

of females prevails in the goose society. . . . The general picture of grief is just as clearly marked in a widowed goose as it is in a dog."

A chimpanzee reacting to the death of his mate made repeated efforts to arouse her; he yelled with rage and expressed his anger by snatching at the short hairs of his head, and then gave way to crying and moaning. Later he became more attached to his keeper than he had been and would become angry if the keeper left him.

Sequence of Behavior

On many levels, animal and human mourning are similar. But there are features of mourning specific to humans—uniquely human responses. Perhaps the most significant of these is the intimate relationship between grief and the intense emotional anxiety caused by separation.

Dr. Spitz's work suggests that when the infant or young child loses his mother he habitually shows responses comparable to pathological mourning in the adult. This observation is also based on studies of healthy children undergoing limited separation in residential nurseries or hospital wards. The predictable three-stage sequence of behavior appears in the separated child. At first, with tears and anger, the child demands the return of his mother and seems hopeful he will succeed in getting her. This phase of *protest* may last days.

In the subsequent periods of *despair* he becomes quieter, but it is clear that he remains preoccupied with his absent mother and still yearns for her return; his hopes, nonetheless, have faded. Often the first two phases alternate: hope turns to despair and despair to renewed hope.

Eventually, however, a greater change occurs. He seems to forget his mother and, when she does come back to him, he is curiously uninterested in her, perhaps not even recognizing her. This is the phase of *detachment.* In each of these phases the child is prone to tantrums and episodes of destructive behavior, often of a disquietingly violent kind. Bowlby believes that there is good reason to believe that this sequence of responses—protest, despair, and detachment—is, in one variant or another, characteristic of all forms of mourning.

When a child loses a mother or father, brother or sister, the psychological effects in the short term are always profound. In many instances a type of personality may develop which either breaks down in later life or is

more vulnerable to breakdown. If the loss of a loved one happens in early childhood, decisive changes in the personality structure often follow. What is critical is the way the matter of the death is handled and whether loving and continuous substitute care is at hand. The emotional scars from such traumatic occurrences appear to be more profound the younger the age of the bereaved.

In Mark's case, for instance, his father and the aunt who took care of him had not realized how important it was that the five-year-old should be encouraged to talk about his mother's death. If Mark had been able to put his fears into words, they would have discovered that he was harboring all sorts of fantasies that he could not cope with, including the fear that he was responsible for his mother's death.

The child often suffers severe guilt if he has had feelings of hostility, even death wishes, against the deceased. If, for example, a brother died, the fantasies of childhood may lead the surviving child to believe that he is responsible. One researcher investigating attitudes of the young towards death quotes two reports by mothers concerning their children's expressions of guilt. "I should have given Tim my tricycle. He wanted it, Mummy. Then he wouldn't have died, would he?" said a six-year-old. "Is it my fault that granny died?" asked an eight-year-old girl. "I didn't carry her bag up the steps."

If an adult finds death difficult to deal with, what might it be for a child who does not comprehend its irreversible consequences and who has such a limited conception both of time and the meaning of separation? Dr. Kliman believes that children should learn about death before it touches their own lives closely.

Buried Pets

A small dose of painful experience, he maintains, "can be mastered by even a very small child. The death of a pet, or even the discovery of a dead bird in the park or the backyard, might provide the first learning experience. Some parents, who have not come to terms with the idea of death themselves, don't—possibly can't—take advantage of such opportunities." As he put it, "Recently I heard a mother shriek, 'Get that thing out of my sight!' when her little girl toddled up to her carrying a dead mouse. Unknowingly, this mother missed a chance to help her daughter absorb the concept of death."

When a pet dies, parents can help

the child cope with his sadness and sense of loss—just by accepting it. Dr. Kliman suggests that parents encourage a child to mourn the pet. A little marker showing where the pet was buried, for instance, will help a child remember the sadness he felt. Simple as this is, it will increase the child's ability to face death and to express his feelings about it.

When someone dies whom the child knew only slightly—a playmate's grandfather, for instance—he should be told about it. He will experience some sadness and he will little by little come to understand some of what his friend feels. When a child loses someone who had been very close—his brother or sister, or worst of all, his mother or father—then the emotional impact is tremendous. This is a critical time. And the way his immediate family reacts, both to the death and to the child, is vitally important.

Most children are not as severely shaken by a death in the family as Mark, but many are. And often the trauma could have been lessened if the parents had prepared the child. Explaining death to children and help-

ing them cope with an actual loss is difficult. But it should not be avoided. If it is handled correctly, the child's emotional development is less liable to suffer. If it is handled incorrectly severe problems may result.

Adults also need help in coping with death. The mourning ritual followed by Orthodox Jews provides a very good example of how this can be done. The period of intensive mourning lasts seven days—corresponding well with the period of intense grief—during which time the mourners, who are supposed to move and do as little as possible, are visited frequently by friends who talk among themselves about the merits of the dead person. The silent, listening mourners find this helps them to concentrate their grief into a short period of time.

After the seven days' intensive mourning the men continue to go to the synagogue twice a day to say a special prayer for the dead for 11 months before the period of mourning is over. This ritual provides the support and reassurance needed, allows grief to be expressed, and imposes a time limit which corresponds with the natural course of grief. Only too often

Grief takes many forms: the first reaction is often numbing shock, followed by wailing and shrieking. The help and support of family and friends is invaluable at this time.

in other communities a bereaved person is put into a kind of purdah—a state of lonely isolation. Wrongly (in most cases) people think mourners wish to be left alone for a long period after their loss.

While grief itself cannot be considered an illness unless it is unduly prolonged or severe, it is undoubtedly associated with a tendency towards illness and death. Studies have shown that recently widowed people fall ill much more often and have a greater mortality rate than groups of single or married people of the same age.

There are many factors which enable people to cope with grief: disturbance of any one of these may mean that the period of mourning is prolonged and intensified to the point of abnormality. And although we can identify many of these factors by observing both animal and human bereavement in general, some are hidden deep within the individual.

Asking the right questions

Interviewing can mean anything from going around a shopping plaza with a clipboard finding out what brands people buy, to asking awkward questions of a celebrity on a TV show. But some of the same aptitudes are involved in all kinds of interview.

Can You Talk to People?

There are "born" interviewers, and others who can learn a lot from special training. Some personalities, however, are unlikely to make good interviewers. To see if you have the necessary personality traits, answer the questionnaire.

1. Do you find that strangers open up and talk to you easily?
a. often
b. sometimes
c. rarely

2. Once someone starts talking to you, can you get him to stop?
a. with great difficulty
b. not without hurting his feelings
c. pretty smoothly, as a rule

3. In conversations, do you talk
a. as much as everyone else?
b. more than everyone else?
c. less than everyone else?

4. Do you watch other people as they talk to you, interpreting their expressions and understanding what they feel?
a. often
b. sometimes
c. rarely

5. Are you soft-hearted?
a. very
b. sometimes
c. not particularly

6. Can you tell if someone is not telling the truth?
a. yes
b. sometimes
c. rarely

7. In a discussion, do you find it hard to stick to the point?
a. rarely
b. sometimes
c. often

8. Have you ever asked a tactless question at the wrong time?
a. seldom
b. not recently
c. frequently

9. Have you been mistaken in your opinion of people?
a. rarely
b. occasionally
c. often

10. Can you assess a person's qualities, setting aside your own feelings about him?

a. usually
b. you hope so, but fear that your judgment may be colored by your feelings
c. it is almost impossible for you to switch off your feelings and give a neutral assessment

How Good is Your Approach?

The art of asking questions is basic to the process of interviewing. Test yourself out on your approach.

1. You are part of a research team investigating child-rearing practices. What you want to know is how much physical discipline is used. Which question(s) would you use?
a. Do you ever spank your little boy?
b. What do you do when your little boy is being really difficult?
c. When did you last spank your child?
d. What sorts of thing would make you spank your little boy?

2. You are interviewing a temperamental actress on a television show. She has recently had a spectacular bust-up with her husband, and no one quite knows what happened. Which question(s) would you use?
a. Is it true that you have split with your husband?
b. Would you like to tell us what really happened with you and your husband?
c. We all know that your husband has left you. Have you anything to say to other women in the same situation?
d. How do you like being free again?

3. You are interviewing a student for admission to a course which involves a lot of close study and difficult reading. He needs to have an interest in books and a critical awareness. Which question(s) would you use?
a. Can you tell us about a book you have read?
b. What are you reading now?
c. Do you enjoy reading?
d. Which book that you have recently read did you most dislike?

---

talent for interviewing.

one at the right time, you may have a you see one. If you can use the right more, you know a good question when possible is **16**. If you scored **10** or Total your scores. The maximum **Scores—a.0, b.2, c.1, d.2.**

but d. is easily the best.

tion b. is more likely to get at the truth, response, and c. is too general. Question a. invites a prepared that you want; a. and c. will give you practically none of the information

3. Questions a. and c. will give you **Scores—a.0, b.1, c.3, d.2.**

saving way to approach the problem. Question d. is a kinder, more face-

likely to call forth a spirited reply. popular, but it would be much more question c. could make you very unanswer. If you ask question b. you also risk a "no comment" response. Using a. could easily lead to a boring than with getting at the truth. Question would make good television, rather ferent. You are concerned with what

2. Here your function is a little different. **Scores—a.0, b.1, c. and d.2.**

up more information. makes the same assumptions, but in a less abrupt way, and it could yield tricked into answering. Question d. does smack her child, so she may be caught off guard. It assumes that she in the Kinsey Report. The subject is Question c. is of the classic type used listen to a lot of irrelevant material. the truth, though you may have to of the mother. You could well get at gests some sympathy for the position is better; it is open-ended and suggests whether or not it is true. Question b. you are likely to be told "never," approved of. If you ask question a, divulge that they do something disapproved of. Mothers are reluctant to situation. You are dealing with a delicate

1. You are dealing with a delicate **Rate Your Approach**

15 indicates little aptitude for the job. just make an interviewer. Less than parts of the questionnaire, you might equally balanced between the two of **15-22** is average; if this score was not answered quite honestly! A score More than that means that you have necessary personality attributes. of **23-29** indicates a high level of the both warmth and judgment. A total you should have scored highly on To be really good at interviewing,

10. a. 2, b. 3, c. 1.
9. a. 3, b. 2, c. 1.
8. a. 3, b. 2, c. 1.
7. a. 3, b. 2, c. 1.
6. a. 3, b. 2, c. 1.

Judgment

desired direction. need to direct the flow of talk in the your warmth could be a handicap; you other hand, if you score more than **12**, demanded by interviewing. On the to make the necessary quick rapport ner may be too distant or shy for you If you have less than **10**, your man-

5. a. 3, b. 2, c. 1.
4. a. 3, b. 2, c. 1.
3. a. 3, b. 2, c. 1.
2. a. 3, b. 2, c. 1.
1. a. 3, b. 2, c. 1.

Personal Warmth

How Do You Rate with People?

Be a better husband

In some societies, marriage is an economic and dynastic arrangement: romantic love is something quite separate. We expect marriage to fulfill both functions—small wonder that we are often disappointed.

Yet our ideal of marriage is attractive. Pair-bonding may be a part of our instinctive nature, so the feeling of coming to rest with one special partner runs very deep.

Are you Satisfied?

Only the lucky or undemanding couples are likely to be completely satisfied with their present marriage. Most of us experience some areas of difficulty, and so it is important to know where the problems lie to make constructive changes. The questionnaire will help you rate your degree of satisfaction, and locate the sources of dissatisfaction. How true are these statements for you?

1. I can talk easily to my wife about the things that are important to me.
a. very true
b. partly true
c. mostly untrue

2. My wife confides in me the things that are important to her.
a. very true
b. partly true
c. mostly untrue

3. When we have a problem, we sit down and talk it over together.
a. nearly always
b. sometimes
c. rarely

4. I like to spend a lot of my leisure time with my wife.
a. very true
b. partly true
c. mostly untrue

5. I can put up with my wife's habits quite happily.
a. usually
b. sometimes
c. with great difficulty

6. My wife puts up with my habits quite happily.
a. usually
b. sometimes
c. with great difficulty

7. Our sex life is very enjoyable.
a. usually
b. sometimes
c. not at all

8. I feel that I "belong" when I'm with my wife.
a. usually
b. sometimes
c. on the contrary, I feel restless and unhappy

9. I rarely get bored when I am with my wife.
a. very true
b. sometimes true
c. untrue

10. I feel reasonably free within my marriage.
a. true
b. sometimes true
c. untrue

Sources of Disharmony

Check off the areas of tension or difficulty in your marriage.

Communication. This is the most important central problem. If honest and clear communication is not taking place, all other difficulties will be magnified. When did you last tell your wife your real thoughts and feelings? You may feel that she is the one who blocks communication between you, but one of you has to make the initial effort if things are to improve. Counseling can help sort out the tangled lines.

Money. This is often symptomatic of personal problems. You may quarrel about money, but what are you really saying to each other? Do you complain about extravagance when you actually resent the fact that your wife stays at home while you work, or that her father makes more than you do? Or when your wife says you don't give her a big enough allowance, is she saying that you don't give her enough appreciation? The feeling of being undervalued is often disguised. You don't have to bring home flowers every day, but try thanking your wife for some of the things she does; notice when she makes an effort; praise her rather than carp at her failures.

Children. They can make or break a marriage. If you quarrel a lot about the children, ask yourself if, in some ways, you resent them. This is a very common feeling. Both wives and husbands can use their children to get at each other. In our society, men usually have less to do with young children and may well feel isolated from them. Talk it out with your wife.

Freedom. However close two people are, they are two people and need to feel that they are individuals as well as part of a couple. Modern marriage demands a degree of freedom for both partners. This can be a real dilemma, because when you love someone, you don't want her to be too free. Freedom does not necessarily mean freedom to have extramarital affairs (though it could mean that) but simply the opportunity to be your own person some of the time. Securing personal freedom has traditionally been more of a problem for women. Are you guilty of tying your wife down? Or does she cling to you in a claustrophobic way? Reluctance to give or take freedom often springs from insecurity. Help her to feel secure; encourage her to be herself. If your insecurity is the trouble, try to get a fresh perspective on yourself.

Sex. What are your expectations of sex? Are they unrealistically high? Are you dogged by puritanical fears? Sex problems in marriage can spring from other problems—it is difficult to become warmly responsive to someone you resent. In general, sex problems are of two kinds: the sexual appetites of the couple can differ, or boredom can set in. Frankness and genuine caring for the other can help in either case. Men and women differ in their needs, but when you can bring out your needs to each other, half the problem has gone. Medical help is also available for every kind of problem, so no situation is hopeless unless you believe it is.

Boredom. One of the reasons for the continued popularity of marriage is that it can be restful, but there is a fine dividing line between peacefulness and boredom. It is natural for people to settle down together; it is also natural for people to seek stimulus. If you both function as individuals, there is less chance of becoming bored, and you each have something to bring back into the marriage. Don't expect to find all your satisfactions from one person. A wife is more likely to give up her friends and career to devote herself to her husband, and so she may narrow her horizons and stagnate. But some husbands make excessive demands of their wives. If you have settled into a dull routine with your wife, it is easy to change it. Surprise her once in a while; go somewhere you've never been before. She will probably follow your example and make life more interesting for you. Boredom is the easiest problem to tackle, for you never really get to the end of a person.

How Do You Rate?

Score 2 for every **a.** answer; 1 for every **b.** answer; 0 for every **c.** answer.

15—20—congratulations! You have a happy marriage.

9—14—you are not too dissatisfied, but there is room for a good deal of improvement in your marriage.

0—8—at present, you are not at all happy about your marriage. Before you resign yourself to it or cut loose, consider how you could improve it.

Be a better wife

You have often been told how to make a better marriage. Get a New Hairstyle. Cook a Different Dish. Pamper the Brute. If that sort of advice works for you, fine. If not you probably want more out of marriage.

Are You Too Romantic?

When a marriage is less than happy, it is often because of faulty, unrealistic expectations. Women are perhaps more likely to suffer from these because our society cherishes the myth that women are longing to get married, while men avoid it until they are "caught." Rate yourself on the questionnaire—you may be more of a romantic than you realize!

1. Do you look at your wedding photographs
a. often?
b. occasionally?
c. you don't even have any?
2. When your husband is preoccupied and fails to notice that you have made a special effort to look good, do you
a. feel hurt, maybe even cry?
b. accept it philosophically?
c. not mind, because you did it for yourself anyway?
3. If you are in the mood to make love, do you
a. act seductive?
b. show affection?
c. invite your husband in a straightforward way?
4. If it becomes clear that you and your husband differ about a political or social issue, would you
a. come around to his point of view?
b. try persuading him to agree with you?
c. go your way and let him go his?
5. Do you find that marriage is
a. much less fun than you thought it would be?
b. pretty much as you expected?
c. more fun than you expected?
6. If your husband were ever unfaithful to you, would you
a. feel totally betrayed and hurt?
b. feel wounded but not mortally, and, anyway, it would depend on the exact circumstances?
c. feel curious about it?
7. Do you wish that your husband would make some effort to be attractive to you?
a. often
b. sometimes
c. rarely
8. If you imagine having an affair with someone, would it be because
a. you want to make your husband jealous?
b. you feel like a change?
c. just because you want to?

Old-fashioned Girls

Traditional marriage leaves only three possible roles for women—the Romantic Wife, the Child Bride, and the Earth Mother. If you are reacting against them, first ask who put you into a stereotype? It wasn't your husband—he thought he was marrying a nice, sexy, companionable human being. It may have been your mother, but you are grown up now.

You are confining yourself. Not consciously, of course. But you carry about in your head a heap of assumptions about what it is to be a wife. You set up a pattern, and you may have regretted it.

Whatever your husband is like, you need to get back to being your own person, and that starts in your head.

Are You Overdependent?

The overdependent wife puts an enormous strain on her husband and children. She lives through them, drinking their vitality, curbing their initiative. Even if they stay, they are likely to feel great resentment and frustration because they cannot be themselves. Still, it is difficult to be loving and protective, yet at the same time not make impossible demands for gratitude and a sense of purpose. Check your dependence rating.

1. When your husband is late coming back from work, and he has not called you up, do you
a. get very anxious and think of all the terrible things that can happen?
b. feel angry with him?
c. stay calm, knowing he must have some reason, and get on with your own activities?
2. You have been invited to a party while your husband is away on business. Do you
a. refuse instantly?
b. go if you know your hosts very well, but feel odd without him?
c. accept and have a good time?
3. You have been offered a job that you would love, but it involves some evening work and your husband would have to get his own supper. Would you
a. turn it down?
b. tentatively talk to your husband about it, and arrange to make it very easy for him if he agrees to your taking the job?
c. take it and expect your husband to share your happiness?
4. Do you call your husband at work about trivial things?
a. often
b. rarely
c. never
5. Do you suggest interesting things to do and places to go?
a. rarely
b. occasionally
c. often
6. Who pays the bills and makes most of the major household decisions?
a. your husband
b. both of you
c. you
7. Your husband has the chance of a sporting holiday and asks if you would mind being left alone for a couple of weeks. Would you
a. feel frightened at the thought?
b. tell him that you'll be fine and send him off?
c. agree, provided that you can have a similar chance?
8. When you get together in the evening, do you
a. expect him to tell you everything that happened to him, since nothing ever happens to you?
b. exchange news, but feel that his is more exciting?
c. exchange news, feeling that your accounts are equally interesting?

How Romantic Are You?

The more as you have, the more romantic you are. More than 5 shows it could be holding you back from making the best of the situation you have. The b scores show a more realistic approach: you reject romanticism, perhaps without knowing what to put in its place. A high c score indicates an antiromantic attitude. Make sure you do not get too hard and suppress your emotions.

Your Dependence Rating

Mainly as (5 or more)—you seem to be too reliant on your husband. Perhaps you think that a wife should live through her husband. Are you convinced that he welcomes your dependence? You will probably find that a little more self-sufficiency and initiative gives him a boost.

Mainly bs (5 or more)—you are breaking out of excessive dependence, although the stereotypes in your head are still there. If you meet resistance from your husband, don't give in or quarrel with him right away. He too needs time to adjust.

Mainly cs (5 or more)—could you be too independent? It could sometimes look like indifference, and your husband may feel rejected. Developing a more democratic relationship would improve your marriage. If you want to be entirely free, why get married?

It makes sense for every wife to be a human being in her own right; that way, she does not make draining demands (or accept them) and she can bring more into the relationship, avoiding the twin traps of resentment and boredom.

Appreciating poetry

Why are we afraid of poetry? It is something we often find embarrassing to admit; we "ought to" enjoy it, but if we are honest we know we do not. There are many reasons for this.

A lot of poetry is difficult to understand, and perhaps it seems unrealistic and irrelevant in the modern world. When you were a student, it may not have been worth the trouble wading through poetry when prose could express the same thoughts more clearly. You were probably bored by it because you felt then that it gave you no information, not even the suspense and excitement of your favorite comics—so why bother?

In fact poems can give you all this and more. Some of them tell our most cherished stories, like this one by Walt Whitman on the death of President Lincoln.

When lilacs last in the dooryard
  bloom'd
And the great star early droop'd
  in the western sky in the night,
I mourn'd, and yet shall mourn with
  ever-returning spring.

It is a basic human need to celebrate great events; if Whitman had said simply, "The spring will always remind me of my grief at Lincoln's death," we would find that only a fraction of our feelings had been expressed.

Reread those lines and you will see just how much more Whitman is saying. The lilacs and the evening star are, in an everyday sense, quite irrelevant to the "story" that the poem is telling, but how essential they are in another sense! They fix the actual moment of grief and so involve you, the reader, in it. More, they suggest that the natural world of flowers and stars is mourning for Lincoln, too. Looked at rationally, this is an absurd idea, yet it gives vent to strong emotions, which are often accompanied by bizarre memories.

Yoking incongruous elements is an important poetic device, and it is a valid concept. Test this for yourself. Think back to a similar important moment: the death of President Kennedy, for instance. You will remember vividly "irrelevant" details charged, like Whitman's lilacs, with chilling significance.

Precious Gift

Poetry is power—it can tap potent feelings we may not even know that we have. In ancient times, this power inherent in words seemed magical. Language was a precious gift and a valuable tool, more complex and useful than any possessed by other living creatures. Words could communicate, impress, control, and skill in combining words effectively was highly prized.

Old spells and magical riddles still retain something of that primitive strength:

In marble halls as white as milk,
Lined with a skin as soft as silk,
Within a fountain crystal clear
A golden apple doth appear.
No doors there are to this
  stronghold,
Yet thieves break in and steal the
  gold.

Words like these could guard secrets, revealed only to those who could understand. The answer to this riddle is—an egg! Poetry still echoes this sense of keeping a secret, another reason why you may have found it difficult at school. But now you can appreciate its subtlety and find pleasure in experiences that are not obvious or banal.

Word of Mouth

You are ready to explore what makes poetry uniquely powerful. First, poetry is durable because rhyme and meter make it easy to remember. Before written records, poets were those who preserved significant events for the whole community, by enshrining them in a memorable pattern of words. Poems—especially the long narrative tales of kings and princes going to war, like the Greek *Iliad* or the Norse sagas—were handed down by word of mouth. They were the community's history, giving it a sense of security and continuity with the past. We all need our experience to be interpreted and reflected by others before we can fully grasp it for ourselves. Poetry is one of the most direct ways of doing this.

The great modern poet T. S. Eliot wrote that it was just as difficult to be precise about feeling as it was about rational thought. If we are not used to confronting our feelings in all their ambivalence, poetry can be threatening. A good poem is good because it is ruthlessly honest and will not let poet or reader off the hook; and a poem is bad not because it is technically incompetent, but because it sentimentalizes, makes difficult things too easy, or gives us only what we expect to hear. That is why the rhymes in greeting cards, for instance, are not poetry.

This does not, of course, mean that good poetry has to be complicated or difficult to understand. The simplicity of these anonymous lines actually makes the feelings expressed all the more poignant:

O Western wind, when wilt thou
  blow
That the small rain down may rain?
Christ! that my love were in my arms,
And I in my bed again.

Being in love is a heightened state of emotion and poetry can express that "special" quality by involving the powerful forces of nature—the wind and the rain—in the personal experience of falling in love. Although we know rationally that our longings do not affect the world around us, feeling that they do is one of the most exciting parts of the experience of love. And that is what the poem brings out for us.

John Donne found that poetry could calm disturbed feelings, too:

Grief brought to numbers cannot
  be so fierce,
For he tames it, that fetters it in
  verse.

Missing Links

By now you will realize that emotional, not rational, order is the aim of poetry. Do not look for cause and effect or logical argument as in prose, but be alert to the emotional resonance of words. Connecting links are often left out, and this can cause problems if the reader is unable to break away from formal patterns of thought.

This old verse works on a "non-logical" basis:

A man of words and not of deeds,
Is like a garden full of weeds;
And when the weeds begin to grow,
It's like a garden full of snow;
And when the snow begins to fall,
It's like a bird upon the wall;
And when the bird away does fly,
It's like an eagle in the sky;
And when the sky begins to crack,
It's like a stick across your back;
And when your back begins to
  smart,
It's like a penknife in your heart;
And when your heart begins to
  bleed,
You're dead and dead and dead
  indeed.

It does not tell an obvious story, but the images develop and become more menacing, leading up to the repeated "dead" in the last line.

Literally, of course, it does not make sense, but emotionally it does. Rational methods and thought processes help us to understand the laws that structure the universe; but poetry gives us the vital psychological sense that we can relate to it in peace and harmony.